GETTING STARTED WITH
WITH
Engineering
Camille McCue, PhD

WILEY

GETTING STARTED WITH ENGINEERING

Published by
John Wiley & Sons, Inc.
111 River Street
Hoboken, NJ 07030-5774

www.wiley.com

CONTENTS

PROJECT 8: ROLLER COASTER MANIA   103

APPENDIX: COOL TOOLS (AND MORE!)   120

INTRODUCTION

SO YOU WANT TO GET STARTED WITH ENGINEERING! Engineers are people who design and invent new products and processes. They improve life by building solutions to problems in the natural world. They use tools and technologies in their daily work. And they team up on projects with scientists, government officials, and business people.

Many grand challenges await you in the world of engineering: making better use of solar energy; creating new types of transportation; securing cyberspace; designing better medicines; providing the world with clean drinking water; applying the function of the brain to computers; inventing new ways to teach people; and improving virtual reality. It's never too early to start, so roll up your sleeves and get ready to work as a junior engineer!

ABOUT THIS BOOK

Engineering is a hands-on field. When you work in engineering, you will use your body as much as you use your brain. In this book, you have opportunities to do both! Sometimes you'll use your eyes and your fingers to work in a small, careful way. An example is using a needle and thread to sew a wearable electronic circuit with LED lights and a battery onto a baseball cap. Other times, you'll use your lungs, legs, and arms to work in a big, athletic way. An example is blowing up balloons to serve as air bags on a Mars lander, and then running up the stairs and hurling the lander off the second floor to (what I hope is) a soft landing on the planetary surface below.

But you'll also use your brain quite a bit. You'll do some online research to learn about engineering projects that have been done before — and how they succeeded or failed. You'll use computer simulations to tinker with a product or a process to learn how it operates. In this way, you can try different ways of building or different ways of conducting a process — before you do them in the real world. You'll brainstorm and draw design plans in your design notebook and then write down how those plans perform and how you can improve them.

Here's what you need to do the projects in this book:

» A computer running a modern version of a Windows or Mac OS X operating system

» A reasonably fast Internet connection

» Some household items, such as foil pans, scissors, a trash bag, tape, a marble, a meter stick, clear plastic wrap, tape, a dog leash, kitty litter, cotton balls, an ear syringe, a thermometer, liquid dishwashing soap, and a kitchen scale (plus a few more items)

» Some food items, such as marshmallows, graham crackers, canola oil, and assorted pasta

» Some home improvement store items, such as foam tubing, PVC elbows, string, sand, and perlite

» Some craft store items, such as craft foam, pipe cleaners, hay, a hot-glue gun, feathers, and faux fur

» One specialty purchase (LilyTwinkle electronics kit for $20) and, optionally, the use of a 3D printer

» Some safety gear, namely goggles, protective gloves, and a face mask

» One design notebook, which can be any notebook with paper or graph paper, to draw designs and write evaluations of your products and processes

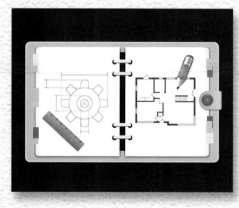

Courtesy of Logovski/Getty

and how to improve them; you can also print photos of your work and paste them into your notebook (optional)

If you're reading this as an ebook, you can click web addresses, such as www.dummies.com, to visit that website.

Every project follows the Engineering Design Cycle, or Engineering Cycle. This process is different from the Scientific Method, which you probably learned in school. I explain the Engineering Cycle in Project 1.

My design sketches are meant to spark your imagination. Your engineering designs may look very much the same or very different from my designs. Your ideas are valuable and I want you to have faith in them. Brainstorm, invent, and build!

Finally, every project wraps up with a section called the Iron Triangle of Engineering. This section helps you think about what real engineers consider when doing that type of project.

ABOUT YOU

Every junior engineer has to start somewhere. When I wrote this book, I assumed that you can

» **Type on a computer and use a mouse.** Your experience can be on a Windows or a Mac system. The simulations you use in this book are computer based (not apps on a mobile device).

» **Read and follow directions.** Each project consists of a sequence of steps to follow. Try to complete the steps mostly as written to get the best results. However, you can make some changes to the steps to match new designs you create.

» **Do a little math and measurement.** Engineers must measure things such as length and mass. In this book, I use the metric system for measurements. Engineers also do computations such as dividing to find a ratio. If you want, you can use a calculator to help you compute. I don't use any formulas, but as you gain new skills you should be ready to use these, too!

» **Follow safety rules and ask an adult for help when you need it.** Engineering is all about safety — putting on your safety gear, looking out for danger, asking for help, and using equipment responsibly. Your development as a junior engineer starts with safe behavior.

» **Bounce back from failure.** *Failure* is a word many grown-ups don't like to say to kids, but it is an important part of engineering. When you design and test ideas, some will succeed and others will fail. Thomas Edison, inventor of the light bulb, said this about failure: "I have not failed 700 times. I have succeeded in proving that those 700 ways will not work. When I have eliminated the ways that will not work, I will find the way that will work."

Courtesy of bilhagolan/Getty

ABOUT THE ICONS

As you read through the projects in this book, you'll see two icons. The icons point out different things:

 This icon marks potential problems or dangers.

 This icon marks helpful information or guidance.

THE FIRST STEP

Whether you view yourself as a future engineer or you just love to tinker and learn new things, your exploration of the projects in this book is a great first step towards fun and rewarding work. Good luck as you enter the world of engineering!

PROJECT 1 ENGINEERING 101

WELCOME TO ENGINEERING! You are beginning an adventure that explores the fun and rewarding field of engineering. Because engineering is not a class most kids see on their school schedules, we'll start with a crash course in Engineering 101.

WHAT IS ENGINEERING?

Engineering is work that uses science, math, and technology to create products and processes. The mission of engineering work is to help humanity and our world. Many times, the goal is to solve an urgent problem, such as building a bridge or setting up a communications network after a disaster. Sometimes, the goal of engineering is to help other living creatures, such as developing *prosthetic* (artificial) legs for a dog born with missing or malformed limbs. Other times, the goal of engineering is to make a process work better and faster, such as scheduling the gates that airplanes use in an airport.

Courtesy of 3D Systems

WHERE DO ENGINEERS WORK?

Engineers work in all types of settings, all over the world. Sometimes engineers work inside, using a computer to design a product. Sometimes they work outside, using special construction equipment to build a structure. Sometimes they work alone, but most of the time engineers work in teams.

Engineers share information with each other when the knowledge and experience of one group can help another group. This was the case when NASA engineers helped the government of Chile rescue 33 miners who were trapped underground. NASA's experience working in hard-to-reach places and in creating rescue capsules contributed to the success in saving the miners.

Courtesy of Hugo Infante/Government of Chile

WHAT ARE SOME ENGINEERING FIELDS?

Many types of engineering exist, and each field offers exciting challenges to solve. Here are a few engineering fields and the products or processes with which they work:

- » **Aerospace:** Build airplanes and spacecraft
- » **Architectural:** Construct buildings, skyscrapers, and landmarks
- » **Biomedical:** Build devices that function with living bodies
- » **Chemical/materials:** Create new products such as medicines, plastics, and fuels
- » **Civil/structural:** Build dams, roads, and bridges
- » **Computer:** Make computers and smart devices
- » **Electrical:** Build electronic equipment; generate and distribute electricity to homes and factories
- » **Environmental:** Focus on pollution control and recycling

» **Entertainment:** Build amusement parks and movie sets

» **Industrial:** Find ways to speed up and improve production lines

» **Marine/ocean:** Design systems to operate in coastal or ocean waters

» **Mechanical:** Design and build machines, including robots

» **Mining/geological:** Focus on mining and earthquakes

» **Nuclear:** Build systems that use the energy of atomic radiation

» **Petroleum:** Find, get, and use oil and natural gas for energy

The Grand Challenges of Engineering are some of the most important work engineers will need to do to help humanity. Learn about them at www.engineeringchallenges.org.

WHAT IS THE ENGINEERING DESIGN CYCLE?

The *Engineering Design Cycle,* or simply, the *Engineering Cycle,* is a set of steps an engineer follows to go from an idea or a need to a manufactured product or a process. When an engineer makes a *product,* such as a spacecraft to go to Mars or a roller coaster, he or she follows this cycle:

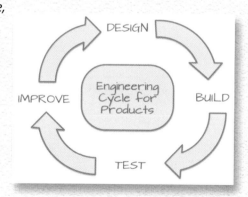

» **Design:** Start with information about a need or a problem, brainstorm ideas on how to solve it, choose one, and then draw how you will make your product in real life.

» **Build:** Use tools and materials to construct your product. A *prototype* is the first build of a product, before it is perfect.

» **Test:** Use your product to find out how well it works.

» **Improve:** Make changes to your product to fix the parts that don't work well.

When an engineer creates a *process,* such as cleaning an ocean oil spill or speeding up the way people move across a bridge, he or she follows this cycle:

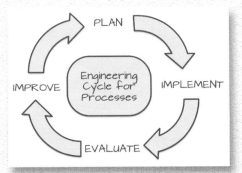

» **Plan:** Start with information about the problem or need, brainstorm ideas about how to address the need, choose one, and then write down the steps for how you will make your proposed process work, start to finish, in real life.

» **Implement:** Perform your process using the steps of your plan.

» **Evaluate:** Decide how well your process works.

» **Improve:** Make changes in your process to speed up or simplify the parts that don't work well.

The Engineering Cycle is a cycle because you continue looping through the steps to constantly improve your product or process.

WHAT DOES A DESIGN LOOK LIKE?

Engineers have special ways of drawing or sketching their designs. They use engineering drawings that show the top, front, and side views of products they build. An example of the top, front, and side views of a proposed building design is shown here. You can use the same method of drawing in your design notebook.

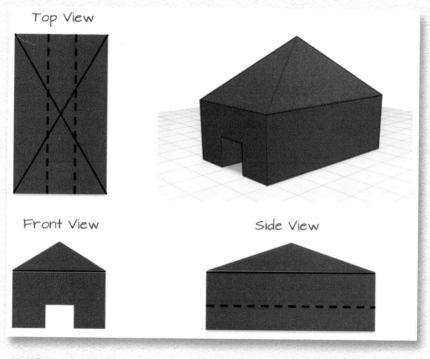

Top View

Front View

Side View

Inventors protect their works by filing patent applications. They include patent drawings like the top-front-side sketches you see here!

Practicing engineering design drawing will be helpful when you create products for 3D printing (see Project 6). A great online game you can play to better understand top, front, and side views is Point of View, which is located at http://pbskids.org/cyberchase/math-games/point-out-view/.

WHAT IS THE GOLDEN RULE OF ENGINEERING?

The *Golden Rule of Engineering* is "keep it simple and double-check your work." This means that the simplest design or plan that meets all the criteria is the best, and that you should carefully check your work before building a design or implementing a plan.

Catching a mistake on paper before it happens in the real world can save money, time, and lives. For example, NASA accidentally burned up its $327 million Mars Climate Orbiter in the atmosphere of the Red Planet when engineers incorrectly used English units instead of metric. The headline in *Wired* magazine read: "Metric Math Mistake Muffed Mars Meteorology Mission."

WHAT IS THE IRON TRIANGLE OF ENGINEERING?

The *Iron Triangle of Engineering* describes three factors engineers must think about when building a product or implementing a process. They must consider:

» **Time:** How fast do they have to get the project done?

» **Features and quality:** How good does the finished product or process have to be?

» **Cost:** How cheap must they be in moving from the idea or need to the completed product or process?

These three factors are related, and it is hard to complete an engineering project that is fast, good, and cheap. Engineers can usually do two of these at one time but not all three, which is typically known as "pick any two."

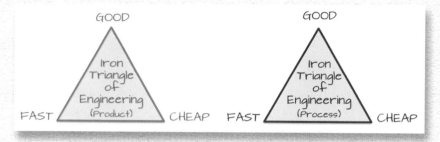

For example, if you want to build a great house quickly, you will have to put more workers on the job, which will cost more money. Or you can make a cheap personal music player and get it in stores fast, but you probably won't have time to perfect it — so quality and reliability may suffer, or it won't as have many features as an expensive music player. As a junior engineer, you consider the Iron Triangle of Engineering in all projects you work on in this book.

MINI PROJECT
CLASSIC POCKET ROCKET

THE CHEMICALLY PROPELLED LAUNCH VEHICLE IS AN OLDIE BUT A GOODIE – AND FUNDAMENTAL TO EVERY KID'S ENGINEERING STUDIES.

Materials: 35mm film canister; water; 6 cm diameter foam circle; goggles; foam triangles, protective gloves, and mask (optional).

Materials to be supervised: Alka-Seltzer tablet; low-temp hot-glue gun and glue; scissors.

DESIGN SKETCH

nose cone

water and Alka-Seltzer in canister

POCKET ROCKET

Design: Sketch the rocket in your design notebook. Your rocket needs a fuel chamber (film canister) and a nose cone to reduce drag during flight. Try different nose cone designs to see how they affect flight! If you want, you can also add fins made from foam triangles.

Warning: Wear goggles (and, optionally, gloves and mask) when working with sharp tools, chemicals, and hot materials!

Build: Construct the nose cone by cutting and removing a wedge from the foam circle. Rotate and hot-glue the cut sides to overlap in a cone, then hot-glue the cone to the rocket at the canister base.

Test: Crumble one Alka-Seltzer tablet and place it in the canister. In an open area outside (and wearing your goggles!), add water to the canister and then quickly cap it. Shake the rocket once and position it upright. Step back a few feet. In 10 to 20 seconds, you'll see an exciting launch! Repeat using different amounts of water to see which makes your rocket go the highest.

Tip: Mixing water and Alka-Seltzer releases carbon dioxide. The gas fills the canister, pushing against the cap to create liftoff.

PROJECT 2 TOUCHDOWN MARS

IN THIS PROJECT, YOUR JUNIOR ENGINEERING JOB CHALLENGES YOU TO DESIGN, BUILD, AND TEST A MARS LANDER. Sending a rover to roll across the surface of the Red Planet requires putting it into a spacecraft package to protect it. This package is a lander that makes a long journey from Earth, followed by entry into the Mars atmosphere, and then a landing on the planet's surface.

You'll build a system that has a parachute to slow the lander in its descent and an air bag system to protect the rover (simulated with an egg) inside the space lander as it hits the ground. You'll also tinker with an online simulation to practice the entry and touchdown process, just like a real NASA engineer. Getting to Mars is one challenge, and landing safely on the surface is another.

Courtesy of NASA

INTRODUCTION TO PLANETARY LANDERS

Did you know that the closest planets to Earth are Venus and Mars — and humans have sent landers to both! The former Soviet Union successfully sent Vega landers to Venus, and the United States landed Viking craft on the surface of Mars.

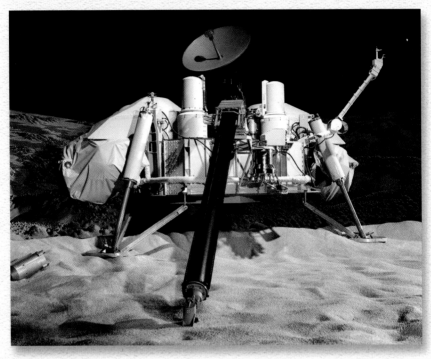

Courtesy of NASA

Venus is full of toxic gases and is probably not a place humans will live in the future. But people may build a space colony on Mars someday. Sending landers there to gather information helps us learn more about the Red Planet.

Rust in Martian rocks makes Mars appear red in the sky — that's why it's called the Red Planet!

The journey of a spacecraft to another planet is long. The shortest time period for going from Earth to Mars is about six months. Traveling fast saves time, but it also means that the spacecraft has to slow down before it can touch down on the surface of Mars.

Learn more about getting from Earth to Mars by reading about the Hohmann transfer orbit.

Aerospace engineers use different ways to slow down vehicles moving through air and space before landing. If you have ever flown on an airplane, you know that an airplane pilot decreases engine speed as you approach the runway. The pilot also extends the wing flaps to increase drag before landing. *Drag* is friction between the wing and the air — the more wing area, the more drag and the more the plane slows down.

Like a plane, a spacecraft must also slow down before landing. You must plan to slow your spacecraft in three places during the landing process:

» **Entry:** When the spacecraft enters the atmosphere of the planet.

» **Descent:** When the spacecraft moves down through the atmosphere to the surface of the planet.

» **Landing:** When the spacecraft touches down on the surface of the planet.

Together, these three phases are called *EDL*.

During descent in the Earth's atmosphere, temperatures on the leading edge of the spacecraft can reach thousands of degrees Kelvin.

MATERIALS

Gather the following materials to conduct your project:

» Protective gear: goggles

» Computer with Internet connection

» Parachute materials: plastic trash bag, string or curling ribbon (a few meters)

» Lander enclosure materials: manila folder, disposable cup, egg carton

» Heat shield (simulated) material: paper or Styrofoam plate *(optional)*

» Cushioning materials: bubble wrap, cotton padding, sponges, packing peanuts

» Air bags: balloons (small to medium size) or zip sandwich bags filled with air

» Hard-boiled egg

» Hole punch

» Duct tape, masking tape, or packing tape

» Meter stick, measuring tape, or ruler

» Permanent marker

» Scissors

SIMULATE A LANDING WITH TECHNOLOGY

It's not easy to land safely on the surface of Mars. A computer *simulation* is a pretend version, using technology, of the real event you want to understand. Using a simulation, you can explore all the ways in which your lander might work — or fail.

PLAY WITH A DESCENT TO MARS

NASA landed Curiosity, a robotic rover about the size of a car, on Mars in 2012. A simulation called Follow Curiosity's Descent to Mars shows the three stages of slowing down a spacecraft (entry, descent, and landing). Play with the simulation at http://mars.nasa.gov/multimedia/interactives/edlcuriosity/index-2.html.

Your role in the simulation is easy: Just click the Play/Pause button to view the lander as it moves towards the surface of Mars. The simulation shows what happens at different altitudes.

Altitude is the height, measured in meters or kilometers, of an object above the planet.

Here's a part of the entry stage at a high altitude. At this stage, the lander is *aerobraking*. Its heat shield is creating drag and getting very hot as it slows down the spacecraft. This process changes *kinetic energy* (the energy of motion) into heat energy.

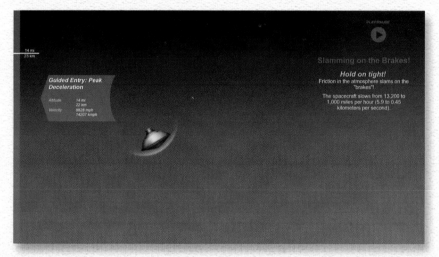

And here is a part of the landing stage at a very low altitude. The lander's Sky Crane is lowering the Curiosity rover to the surface.

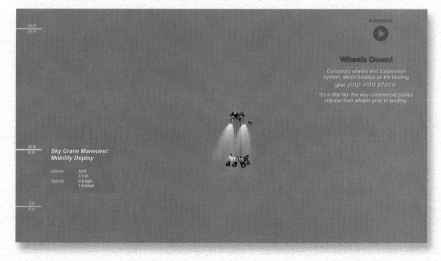

The Sky Crane uses *retrorockets* (rockets that fire to slow down, not to lift off) to hover. It also uses cables to lower the rover for a soft landing. Hard landing methods use cushions such as air bags to drop and bounce onto the planetary surface.

CONTROL A DESCENT TO MARS

The Curiosity Landing Simulation puts you in the role of a flight controller. Your job is to set the parameters to land the Curiosity rover on Mars. *Parameters* are things you can change, such as

» The angle at which you approach the surface of the planet. Moving parallel to the ground is 0 degrees. A direct dive is 90 degrees.

» The time at which to *deploy* (pop open) the parachute.

» The time at which to *jettison* (remove) the heat shield.

» The time at which to use the Sky Crane to lower the rover.

Play with the simulation at www.khanacademy.org/partner-content/nasa/searchingforlife/mars_science_lab/p/curiosity-landing-simulation.

This simulation runs like a game. Hover your cursor over a slider to learn more about a landing parameter. Then slide the slider bar to set a value for that parameter. After you have set all the parameters, click the Start Entry! button.

Curiosity Landing Parameters

Angle of attack: 16°
SUFR: 1238 m/s
Parachute: 3:31
Heatshield: 4:03
Backshell: 1800 m
Freefall: 0:04
Constant velocity: 90 m
Skycrane: 20 m

Start Entry!

The simulation starts the EDL process. It shows your time, altitude, and other information about what is happening as your lander moves towards Mars. At any time, click the Abort button to halt the mission.

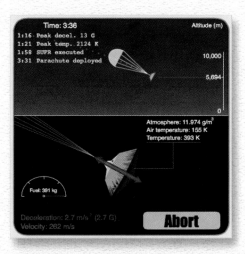

Don't be discouraged if your parachute burns up or you crash on the first few attempts! With practice, you will decide on parameter values that will successfully land the rover on Mars.

It can take many tries to get the right balance of parameters to safely land Curiosity. That's why you use a simulation — to figure out all the places where your engineering design may fail so that it most likely won't fail when you run the mission in the real world!

DESIGN YOUR MARS LANDER

After you have run a successful Mars landing on the computer, you will know a little more about designing a Mars lander in the real world. Your lander will be a small model of a real lander (because it won't actually go to Mars) and will transport a pretend rover in the form of an egg. Plan to land the egg rover — without cracking it! — as it descends from a 4-meter altitude to the ground.

Beginning with the design phase of the Engineering Cycle, draw on paper a design for your lander.

What stages of EDL (entry, descent, and landing) can you work on? Think about how you will plan each stage:

Courtesy of iStockphoto

» **Entry:** How will you adjust the entry angle of your lander? Will you drop the lander? Will you toss it horizontally so that it moves forward as it is falling? Or will you do something in between?

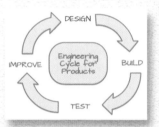

» **Descent:** How will you slow your lander as it falls? Will you add a parachute? Can you design a parachute out of a trash bag and string?

» **Landing:** How will you make your lander land? You will have to plan for a hard landing, but what materials can you use to soften it? Can you make the cushioning materials easy to remove so that the rover can exit quickly after landing?

When you sketch your design, label the materials you plan to use. Also show the *dimensions* (the sizes) of each part of your lander.

A 4-meter drop is about arm height on a second-floor balcony. This altitude works well as the starting point for the entry stage of your Mars lander.

Your design sketch may not look like the one shown here. You may choose to make a box shape or use a cup as the main lander enclosure. Or you may choose something completely different. It's your design, your choice!

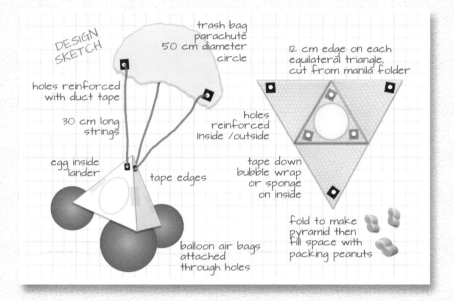

DESIGN SKETCH

trash bag parachute 50 cm diameter circle

holes reinforced with duct tape

30 cm long strings

egg inside lander

tape edges

12 cm edge on each equilateral triangle, cut from manila folder

holes reinforced Inside /outside

tape down bubble wrap or sponge on inside

fold to make pyramid then fill space with packing peanuts

balloon air bags attached through holes

BUILD YOUR MARS LANDER

The next phase of the Engineering Cycle is the build phase. Here, you construct your Mars lander.

Gather your materials, put on your goggles, and begin the building process.

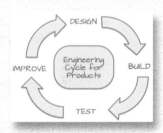

1 **With adult supervision, hard boil two or three eggs.**

Using hard-boiled eggs will reduce the mess of a lander failure (a cracked egg).

2 **Use scissors, a pencil, a ruler, and a manila folder to construct a landing lander.**

Cut a net of a pyramid or a cube that can be folded to contain the egg rover. A **net** is a two-dimensional pattern you can cut and fold to make a three-dimensional shape. Or you may choose to keep it simple by using a disposable cup or an egg carton cup to surround the egg.

Check that the egg rover fits easily inside the lander before adding cushioning materials. Too snug of a fit may make it hard to add cushioning, and the egg might not get the protection it needs to survive impact. Too much extra space means you will need lots of cushioning to fill the gap, which increases the weight at launch — an expense you want to avoid.

3 Add cushioning materials to the inside of the lander.

Cut layers of bubble wrap or other padding to line the lander. Tape down the padding. Make sure that the egg still fits as you add layers. Try to keep the layers fluffy so that they help the egg rover survive the impact of landing.

4 At the top of the lander, create three or four attachment points for your parachute.

For each attachment point, cut a square of duct tape, about 1 cm by 1 cm. Place the duct tape squares where you will attach your parachute strings. Punch a hole in each square, all the way through the lander.

5 Use scissors, a permanent marker, a ruler, and a trash bag to construct a parachute.

Spread out the trash bag on a flat surface. Mark a spot on the bag at about the center. Measure out 25 cm from the spot, in any direction, and mark a dot. Repeat this several times in different directions. The dots should roughly form a circle. Draw the circle and then cut it out to create your parachute.

6 Around the edge of your parachute, create three or four attachment points for your strings.

For each attachment point, cut a square of duct tape, about 1 cm by 1 cm. Place the duct tape squares where you will attach your parachute strings. Punch a hole in each square, all the way through the parachute.

7 **On the base of the lander, create three or four attachment points for your air bags.**

For each attachment point, cut a square of duct tape, about 1 cm by 1 cm. Place the duct tape squares where you will attach your air bags. Punch a hole in each square, all the way through the lander.

8 **Attach the air bags to the lander.**

Blow up three or four small balloons, tying off the end of each balloon. For each balloon, poke the tied-off end through the hole in the base of the lander. Inside the lander, use duct tape to secure the end of the balloon. Repeat this process for each balloon.

Air bags increase the time its takes for the lander to change from moving to stopped. This decreases the force felt by the contents of the lander, the egg. In the same way, air bags in cars protect the people inside from injury during a crash.

9 **Insert the egg rover and add more cushioning into the lander.**

Place the egg into the lander. If you created a pyramid or cube net, fold up the edges of the lander container. Add packing peanuts or any other cushioning you want around the egg. Tape the sides shut with masking tape or painter's tape. Avoid using duct tape because it will be too hard to reopen the lander to check for egg cracks after the test.

10 **Attach the parachute to the lander.**

Cut three or four lengths of string or curling ribbon. Use any length you want; a 30 cm length works well. Insert one end of a string through a parachute hole and the other end through a hole at the top of the lander. Tie the string at each end to secure it. Repeat this process for each of the other strings.

TEST YOUR MARS LANDER

It is now time for the test phase of the Engineering Cycle. With adult help, find a place where you can release your lander at an altitude of around 4 meters. The balcony of a two-story house works well. Pack your parachute into a wad prior to testing. Release your lander into the air

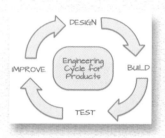

by dropping it or throwing it horizontally, depending on what you planned during the design phase. Evaluate how your lander performs during its entry, descent, and landing.

In your design notebook, sketch the EDL flight and make notes about each stage:

1 **For entry, note the angle of release into the air.**

2 **For descent, write about the performance of the parachute.**

How well did it open? Did it slow the fall of the lander?

3 **For landing, was your egg rover damaged (cracked) or safe (uncracked)?**

Were the air bags placed in positions where they softened lander impact?

Your observations of how the lander performs in each phase will help you during the improve phase of the Engineering Cycle.

If your lander functions without failure, try releasing it from a higher altitude. You may want to throw it upwards so that it begins its entry from more than 4 m above the ground.

IMPROVE YOUR MARS LANDER

In the improve phase of the Engineering Cycle, your goal is to learn from what worked and what failed during the test phase. Can you make a few small changes to improve your design? Is there a way to make it easier to load and unload the egg rover from the lander? Can you reduce the mass of the lander and still keep the egg from cracking?

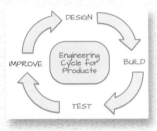

Many nations are working on engineering landers to send to Mars and other planets. The information learned by engineers on each new mission helps other engineers build better landers in the future. Your efforts in designing, building, testing, and improving this junior engineering version of a Mars lander may someday lead to new tools for visiting unexplored planets!

The lander's tetrahedron (pyramid) shape helps it to right itself if it lands on it side. Read more about this process online!

AEROSPACE ENGINEERING AND THE IRON TRIANGLE

As you wrap up your work in engineering a planetary lander, think about the big picture of working on an aerospace engineering project. The Iron Triangle of Engineering tells us that we want to do a

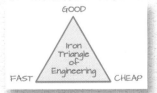

good job, as fast as possible, at a cheap cost, but that only two of the three can actually be accomplished.

Aerospace engineering projects must be good, but this can be hard to guarantee because the work is complex. Space projects are new and different from each other and we have no easy way to test every part of a project here on Earth. Even with the best planning, some aerospace missions fail. However, other aerospace products such as airplanes must be good (reliable) at all times to keep their passengers safe.

It is not easy to decide on how important fast is when it comes to aerospace projects. Some projects must be done quickly because they meet important human needs. Launching communications satellites and weather satellites into orbit are examples of such needs. But these needs may not be critical compared to other human needs such as having safe drinking water. At the same time, engineering planetary landers is important for humans to understand our universe and someday build colonies away from Earth. This could be critical for the future of humanity.

Aerospace engineering is usually not cheap. Airplanes and rockets are large, complicated devices that take a lot of planning, special materials, building time, and testing time to produce. Some aerospace engineering work, such as making planes, may earn money back because people will pay for commercial flights. But space exploration projects can cost millions of dollars — and people may not see the payoff of this work right away.

Which two items on the Iron Triangle of Engineering do you believe are most important to an aerospace engineering project and why?

PROJECT **3** THE CLOCK IS TICKING

IS INDUSTRIAL ENGINEERING AN UNFAMILIAR ENGINEERING FIELD? When you schedule your homework, plan what you want to do on vacation, clean the clutter from your backpack, arrange your clothes, or figure out the most efficient route to ride your bike to school, you are working as an industrial engineer!

Industrial engineering is about *optimization* — finding the best, fastest, and cheapest way to get a product made or a process completed. In this project, you learn how to build a simple *Gantt chart* (time-planning chart) to schedule a set of tasks, and then you use it to solve a fun problem: getting people who walk at different rates across a bridge at night before their lamp burns out.

Courtesy of Tashatuvango/Shutterstock

ALL HERE, IN ORDER, ON TIME. LET'S GO!

Railroads such as Amtrak need industrial engineers to schedule trains, cargo, passengers, conductors, and maintenance technicians round the clock. Companies that warehouse billions of items and process millions of orders every day, such as Amazon, also rely on industrial engineers to organize their activities.

Courtesy of the Collection of Doug Helton, NOAA/NOS/ORR

Industrial engineering focuses on *logistics,* which is the coordination of people, facilities, and supplies. An industrial engineer works to *optimize* (make the best use of) time and resources. Here are some tasks an industrial engineer performs:

» **Watch and learn:** Observe a process start to finish to understand how it works and how well it works.

» **Communicate:** Talk with people who will use the product or service to understand the goal of the work.

» **Plan facilities:** Set up the location and layout of manufacturing facilities (places that make things) and warehouses (places that store things).

» **Schedule:** Plan the time needed to make a product or carry out a process.

» **Staff:** Hire or train people, and use robots and computers in jobs that don't need people.

» **Get supplies and construct:** Find or make parts that are assembled into a larger product, making sure that those parts are available in the right amounts when they are needed.

» **Manage operations:** Plan how all the parts of production or process fit together, keeping costs and *turnaround* (the time it takes to get something done) as small as possible.

» **Control quality:** Check for mistakes in products, and figure out from the number of mistakes when a bigger production problem has occurred (such as a broken machine). Fix the process or systems to make sure these problems do not occur again.

In this project, you play the role of an industrial engineer. You design and implement a process for getting a group of people across a bridge. But this task has some *constraints* — things that limit the way in which you can get the job done. You will apply the Engineering Cycle for Processes outlined in Project 1. You may have to evaluate and improve your process a few times before you can complete the task with success!

 Figuring out whether a change has occurred in a process — and when the change took place — is a field called change point detection.

MATERIALS

To conduct this project, you will need

» Computer with an Internet connection

» Grid paper

» Colored pencils

SIMULATE A SIMPLE LOGISTICS PROCESS

Before you work a hard problem, it's a good idea to work on a similar but easier problem. When you succeed in solving the easy problem, you'll be prepared to move on to more difficult problems with additional constraints. For example, when you learn multiplication tables, you first work to solve the problems correctly, and then you add a time constraint so that you have to get the right answers fast.

You'll first solve an easy logistical process, and then move on to a more challenging process. The simple process is a famous puzzle called Wolf, Sheep, and Cabbage.

Open the computer simulation called Wolf, Sheep, and Cabbage at www.plastelina.net/game1.html. The simulation shows a man in a boat at the edge of a riverbank, where a wolf, a sheep, and a box of cabbage sit. The man can transport only one item at a time (besides himself) across the river. He can also cross alone, without any item in the boat.

Your job is to help him take all three items across the river. But be aware that if the man is not there to keep watch, the sheep will eat the cabbage — or the wolf will eat the sheep!

Complete these steps to simulate the transportation process:

1 Click the Play button to begin.

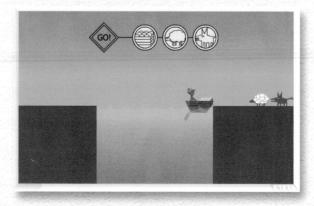

2 **Click the icon (the round button) of the item you want to load into the boat, and then click the Go! button.**

The item is loaded into the boat, and then the man rows the item across the river. Click the Go! button without an item in the boat to make the man cross the river alone.

3 **If the boat completes its river crossing, click the item icon again (when you reach the riverbank) to unload the item from the boat.**

The item moves from the boat to the riverbank.

4 **If the sheep eats the cabbage or the wolf eats the sheep, click the Try again! button that appears.**

The action restarts, so you can make changes and try again.

5 **Repeat Steps 2 to 4 in varying combinations until all the items have been moved across the river.**

When you are successful at moving all the items across the river, a *Well Done!* message appears.

Items can be moved back and forth across the river as many times as you want. Try taking the sheep across first. The solution will include more than one journey for the sheep!

SIMULATE A MORE COMPLEX LOGISTICS PROCESS

In Wolf, Sheep, and Cabbage, you worked like an industrial engineer, focused on where to move items and when to move them. In that simulation, there was no time constraint. You will now work on a more complex logistics process.

Your new challenge, a simulation called the Family Crisis, includes time constraints. Open the simulation at www.plastelina.net/game3.html.

In Family Crisis, a family of five is stranded during the night on the right side of a cliff. You help walk them across a log bridge before their lantern fades out. No more than two people can walk across the bridge at a time. Someone must carry the lamp on every crossing. If the lamp burns out, the people can't see where they're walking and are in danger of falling.

Each person takes a different amount of time to cross the log bridge:

» Athlete: 1 second

» Average Joe: 3 seconds

» Girl: 6 seconds

» Photographer: 8 seconds

» Grandpa: 12 seconds

The process has two time constraints:

» If two people cross the log together, they walk at the speed of the slower person.

» The lamp has only 30 seconds of light.

Complete these steps to try out the simulated log crossing process:

1 **Click the Play button to begin.**

2 **Click the icon (the diamond button) of each person you want to cross the log.**

The icon for each person is highlighted. To remove a person, click his or her icon again.

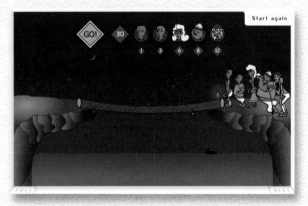

3 **Click the Go! button.**

The selected person or people cross the log at the speed of the slower person. The clock shows the number of seconds of lamp use remaining.

4 **If time remains on the clock, repeat Steps 2 and 3.**

5 **If you run out of time and the lamp burns out, click the Try again! button that appears.**

The process restarts, so you can make changes and try again. Note that you can click the Start again button at any time — you don't have to wait until the lamp burns out to try a different process.

PLAN YOUR INDUSTRIAL ENGINEERING PROCESS

Moving the family across the log given the time constraints requires good logistics. The Engineering Cycle for Processes gives you a method to plan, implement, evaluate, and improve these logistics.

In the first phase of the cycle, planning, you work to understand the parts of the process and the constraints. You then propose ways to carry out the process successfully — *before* you take any action in the real world.

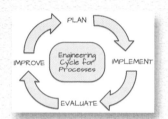

As a junior industrial engineer, you will want to use a tool such as a Gantt chart to help you plan the logistics of Family Crisis.

PLAN WITH A GANTT CHART

A *Gantt chart* is a planning tool that engineers use to make a schedule. Use grid paper and colored pencils to make a Gantt chart as follows:

1 **List all the different tasks that take place in the process.**

For Family Crisis, a task is a person walking across the log. List these down the left side of the grid. Use a different color for each task.

GANTT
CHART

Athlete
Average Joe
Girl
Photographer
Grandpa

2 Create the timeline for the process from start to finish.

Family Crisis must be completed in 30 seconds, so list the number of seconds from 30 to 1 across the top of the grid.

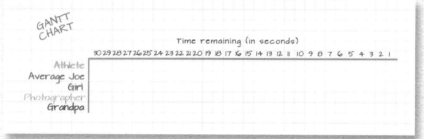

GANTT
CHART

Time remaining (in seconds)
30 29 28 27 26 25 24 23 22 21 20 19 18 17 16 15 14 13 12 11 10 9 8 7 6 5 4 3 2 1

Athlete
Average Joe
Girl
Photographer
Grandpa

3 For each task, shade in the time span when that task takes place.

This chart shows that the first crossing is by the Athlete and the Average Joe. The Athlete could cross in 1 second, but he is constrained by Joe, who requires 3 seconds. These *concurrent tasks* take place at the same time.

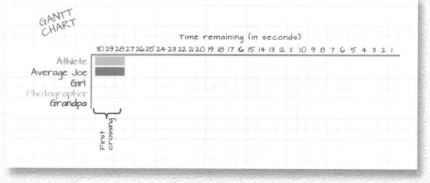

GANTT
CHART

Time remaining (in seconds)
30 29 28 27 26 25 24 23 22 21 20 19 18 17 16 15 14 13 12 11 10 9 8 7 6 5 4 3 2 1

Athlete
Average Joe
Girl
Photographer
Grandpa

First crossing

4 **Repeat Step 3, moving along the timeline until the process is complete.**

This chart shows that the second crossing is by the Athlete alone. It then shows that the third crossing by the Athlete and the Girl. The chart continues, showing a plan in which the Athlete goes across with each person, and then returns to get the next person. As you can see, in this plan, time runs out before the Athlete and Grandpa complete their crossing!

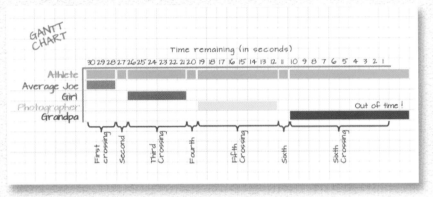

5 **Revise the planning until you create a sequence that appears to move the family across within the 30-second time period.**

PLAN BY ACTING IT OUT

Another way to plan the logistics of a problem is to act it out. Gather five people or find five stuffed animals to play the roles of the family members. Create a log with a pool noodle and role-play the problem in real life. Try walking the family members in different orders — and with different pairs of concurrent walkers — to create a plan that completes the process in the time allowed.

BUILDING A HOUSE

A construction engineer uses a Gantt chart when planning the building of a house. The chart shows the pouring of the foundation, the framing of the structure, the plumbing, the wiring of the electrical, the drywall installation, the painting, the roofing, and other tasks. The chart also shows the date when the task will start, and how many days or weeks it will take to complete the task. Some tasks cannot happen at the same time as other tasks. For example, the foundation must be poured before the walls are framed. Other tasks can be concurrent. For example, tile can be installed inside the house while the outside of the house is painted. Constraints in building a home can include bad weather, construction crews not arriving for work, and delays in receiving materials. But careful creation of the Gantt chart can get the home built as fast as possible. This means the home buyer can begin living in the home sooner and the home builder can make money from the sale more quickly!

IMPLEMENT YOUR LOGISTICAL PLAN

With your Gantt chart in hand, return to the Family Crisis simulation on the computer and then implement the plan you developed. Carefully follow your steps, and note whether the timer matches your chart following each crossing.

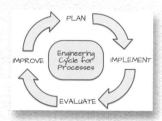

SUPER SIDEWALKS OF LONDON

Using a Gantt chart can help transportation engineers optimize the motion of people in transit around a city. Such a chart is especially important in predicting the use of new designs in public transportation.

An exciting idea in London is that of replacing subways with a series of moving sidewalks. An architectural firm has proposed removing the Circle Line subway (which is often delayed and packed with tourists) and installing three side-by-side walkways moving at different speeds. A passenger would step onto a sidewalk moving at 5 kilometers per hour (around 3 miles per hour), then step over to a sidewalk moving at 10 kph, and finally step over to one moving at 15 kph. Between stations, the sidewalks could speed up to 25 kph! By getting rid of the need to stop at each station, a passenger could complete the full circle in 55 minutes — 5 minutes faster than the train. And for passengers with mobility equipment, such as a wheelchair or a baby carriage, the difficulty of getting into and out of a subway car is eliminated.

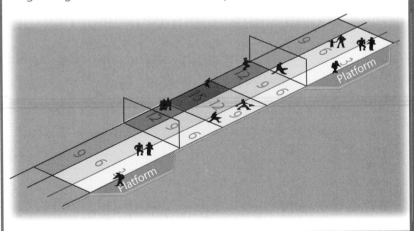

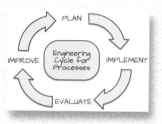

EVALUATE YOUR SUCCESS

Evaluating your success as an industrial engineer means deciding how well you set up logistics given the constraints. In Family Crisis, this means walking the family across the log before the lamp goes out. You are successful if you meet or beat the 30-second deadline.

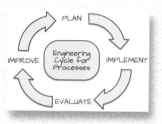

IMPROVE YOUR PROCESS

Improving your logistics in industrial engineering means revising plans until you create successful processes. In Family Crisis, this means improving your Gantt chart until you have a plan that transports the family within 30 seconds.

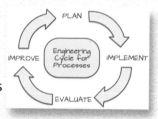

Don't erase or throw away plans that didn't work. Finding out what fails is just as important as finding out what works. If you know what fails, you know to avoid using that same process again. You may need to revise your process many times (using lots of grid paper!) until you come up with a plan that works.

When you are successful, a *Perfect!!!* message appears. If you want, click the Play again button to restart the process and try other possible combinations.

A good way to save time and speed up the process is to walk the slowest family members concurrently.

IRON TRIANGLE OF ENGINEERING

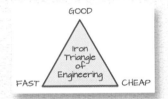

Industrial engineers consider the Iron Triangle of Engineering in every logistical process they develop. The Iron Triangle says that we can do only two out of the following three things: create a good process (the logistics run well), create a process that operates fast, and create a process that is cheap. However, more than any other type of engineer, an industrial engineer believes that you really can do all three! The main point of the industrial engineer's job is to plan and implement logistics that make processes run at *optimal* (the very best) levels.

If you can multitask, create great work products, and stretch your allowance further than your friends, industrial engineering may be a career for you!

GANTT CHARTING WITH A SPREADSHEET

A spreadsheet is a great tool to use for creating a Gantt chart. Numbers for Mac, Microsoft Excel, and Google Sheets are all easy-to-use spreadsheets. Each one gives you a simple way to list tasks and show start and stop times for each task in a digital format. One benefit of using a digital format is that you can rearrange tasks and adjust time spans quickly, unlike when using a chart on paper. Spoiler alert: The Google Sheets document shown here has a successful solution to Family Crisis!

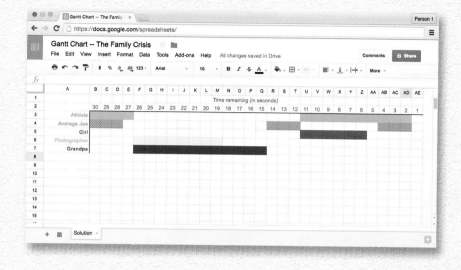

PROJECT 4 SQUEAKY CLEAN UP

SQUEAKY CLEAN UP INVITES JUNIOR ENGINEERS TO RESPOND TO AN ENVIRONMENTAL DISASTER – AN OIL SPILL. Drilling into the ground and ocean floor is usually safe, but sometimes a spill occurs. In this project, you'll simulate an ocean oil spill. Then you'll race to contain it and remove the oil from the surrounding water, testing a variety of containment and cleaning materials.

Courtesy of Ron Wooten, Platform Observer/Whale Watch, Galveston Lab, National Marine Fisheries Service/National Oceanic and Atmospheric Administration/Department of Commerce

INTRODUCTION TO OIL SPILL CLEAN UPS

The demand for fossil fuels such as crude oil to power our world is high. Some oil is located below land. Other oil can be found under shallow or deep water. However, removing the oil so that it can be used is not easy. Sometimes oil spills can occur, due to human mistakes.

An *oil spill* occurs when liquid petroleum is released into the environment. When a drill bores into the ground or the ocean floor, there is always a risk of a spill. A spill on land is a mess, but like an oil spill on your kitchen floor, it doesn't move around as you're cleaning it up. An oil spill in the water moves with the water, spreading quickly.

An ocean oil spill can also happen when a transport ship carrying oil hits an obstacle. This can cause the ship's hull to rip open and leak its contents.

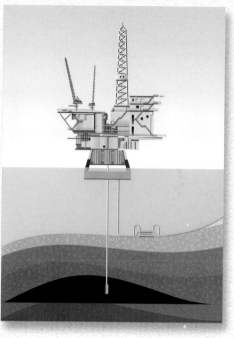

Courtesy of Youst/Getty

One of the worst ocean oil spills resulted from an explosion on British Petroleum's Deepwater Horizon rig in the Gulf of Mexico in 2010. About 780 million liters leaked from the well during the 85 days it took to plug the leak.

Whether an ocean oil spill occurs due to a drilling accident or a collision, engineers must act quickly to fix the problem. Otherwise, ocean currents, waves, winds, and tides will spread the oil out into a larger area, making it harder to clean up.

In this project, you will design and implement a process for containing and cleaning an oil spill, applying the Engineering

Cycle for Processes outlined in Project 1. Following your clean-up attempt, you will evaluate your process and consider ways to make it better.

MATERIALS

Gather the following materials to conduct your project:

» Protective gear: goggles, household cleaning gloves, mask to cover mouth (optional)

» Old newspapers

» Canola oil (1/2 cup)

» Oil-based food coloring (red): must be an oil candy color dye such as a Wilton or Americolor product; standard food coloring from the supermarket will not dissolve in oil

» Disposable cup

» Ocean pan: disposable foil roasting pan (large)

» Waste pan: disposable foil pie pan (small)

» Water: enough to fill about half the roasting pan

» Salt: enough for a few sprinkles

» Barriers: any of Popsicle sticks, wooden stir sticks, cotton rolls, pipe cleaners (8); string (about 1 meter) or modeling clay (a handful)

» Scissors

» Skimmers: eyedropper with a suction top, or a pipette, or an ear bulb syringe

» Nylon pantyhose (1 pair)

- » Organic sorbents: any of peat moss, straw, hay, sawdust, ground corncobs (one handful of each)

- » Inorganic sorbents: sand, clay, kitty litter, perlite (one handful of each)

- » Plastic spoon

- » Liquid dishwashing soap (2 tablespoons)

Most of the supplies for this project can be found at a nursery, a home and garden store, or a big box hardware store.

PLAN YOUR OIL SPILL CLEAN-UP PROCESS

Later in this project, you will make an oil spill and then clean it up. Start the Engineering Cycle for Processes by planning the process you will use to conduct clean up.

As you plan, think about what methods and tools you will use to clean up the oil spill. Some options to consider are

- » Contain the oil.

- » Skim (suck up) the oil.

- » Use sorbents (materials that collect another substance).

- » Disperse (break up) the oil.

Let's look at each option more closely.

PLAN TO CONTAIN THE OIL

Containing the oil means placing a barrier around it so that the oil cannot move and spread across the ocean surface. Barriers can just block the flow of oil (*hard booms*) or they can also absorb the oil (*sorbent booms*). Try using Popsicle sticks, string, or pipe cleaners as a containment

Courtesy of the Collection of Doug Helton, NOAA/NOS/ORR

barrier. You might also want to try using cotton rolls as oil-absorbing barriers.

PLAN TO SKIM THE OIL

Skimming the oil means collecting it directly out of the water by sucking or suctioning it. A *skimmer* is a device that performs this suction job. Try using an eyedropper, a pipette, or an ear syringe to suction the oil from the water.

PLAN TO USE SORBENTS

Sorbents are materials that adsorb or absorb. They are used to remove the oil that skimmers cannot suck up. To work well in cleaning oil spills, sorbents must be able to both attract oil and repel water.

Most sorbents used for oil spill clean ups are *adsorbent:* They attract oil so that it clings to their surfaces. *Organic adsorbents* are used on the surface of the water and can attract from 3 to 15 times their weight in oil. Try peat moss, straw, hay, sawdust, and ground corncobs. *Inorganic adsorbents* are used below the surface of the water and can attract from 4 to 20 times their weight in oil. Try sand, clay, kitty litter, and perlite (a volcanic glass used with plant potting mixes). Man-made adsorbents, such as plastics, can also be used to attract oil.

Organic means the material was once living, such as hay, which was once grass. *Inorganic* means the material never lived, such as sand. Both organic and inorganic materials are found in nature. Man-made materials, which are not naturally found, are also called *synthetic*.

Some sorbents used for oil spill clean up are *absorbent:* They pull the oil into the material. These absorbents are mostly man-made because they have to be chemically engineered to soak up more oil than water. Man-made absorbents include a type of rubber. Some of these materials can soak up to 70 times their weight in oil!

Sorbents are often in the form of loose particles. You can try sprinkling them directly onto an oil spill, keeping track of how much you use. After loose sorbents have had a chance to attract remaining oil, they may be scooped up. In this project, you can use a plastic spoon to do this collection. Another way to use sorbents is to put them into a net or mesh sack to use during oil collection. Try cutting a section of pantyhose to create such a sack.

PLAN TO DISPERSE THE OIL

One method that some clean-up crews have used with ocean oil spills is the opposite of concentrating and collecting it. They *disperse* it, or break up the oil into smaller gobs that can then be spread out over a larger area. The idea is like putting dish soap on a greasy pan to clean it.

Courtesy of Technical Sergeant Adrian Cadiz, USAF Photo

The materials used to make the oil break up are called *dispersants*. They can be sprayed from an airplane over the water or applied from nozzles on hoses attached to ships or trucks, similar to crop dusting!

Dispersed oil doesn't stay on the surface in a slick; it falls as droplets into the ocean depths. Then the motion of the ocean breaks up the oil droplets even more so that the toxic chemicals in the oil are spread out over a much larger volume of water. In this project, try dispersing the simulated oil spill by adding a drop of dishwashing soap to the spill and seeing what happens.

Dispersants may create more problems than they solve. Some dispersants are made of chemicals that are just as toxic to the environment as the oil spill itself.

SKETCH YOUR PROCESS

After you gather materials and consider how you will use them in cleaning up the simulated spill, sketch out your planned process. Create a simple numbered list to show the order of the steps you plan to take and the materials you will use to perform each step. Be sure to note what you will do with the waste oil and clean-up materials as you take these out of the water.

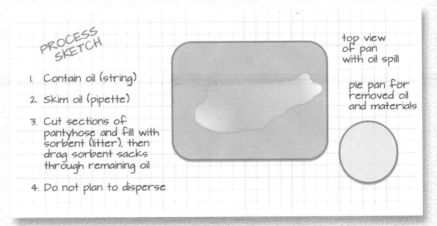

PROCESS SKETCH

1. Contain oil (string)

2. Skim oil (pipette)

3. Cut sections of pantyhose and fill with sorbent (litter), then drag sorbent sacks through remaining oil

4. Do not plan to disperse

top view of pan with oil spill

pie pan for removed oil and materials

IMPLEMENT YOUR CLEAN-UP PROCESS

Take all necessary safety precautions to protect your eyes, nose, mouth, and hands before you begin working with the materials. Wear your goggles and gloves when working with sharp tools and chemicals. You might also want to wear a facemask when working with materials such as hay and sawdust to reduce the inhalation of these items.

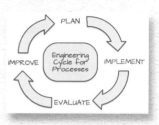

Spread newspapers on your work area to protect it. Make sure you have your materials and your process sketch handy before you begin implementing your clean-up process.

SIMULATE THE OIL SPILL

Complete these steps to simulate an oil spill:

1 Create the oil (liquid petroleum).

Mix the canola oil and 3-4 drops of oil-based red food coloring with a plastic spoon in a disposable cup.

2 Create the ocean.

Fill the disposable roasting pan halfway with water and then stir in several sprinkles of salt. Mix to dissolve the salt.

3 Spill the oil into the ocean!

 Oil can be a variety of colors: transparent, yellow, red, brown, or black, depending on exactly what is in it.

EXECUTE YOUR CLEAN-UP PLAN

Complete the steps you created in your clean-up plan. Remember, you don't have to use every type of clean-up method. You may have the same steps or different steps than those shown here.

1 Contain the spread of the oil spill.

Use your containment materials to create a barrier between the oil and the ocean.

2 Skim the oil.

Use your skimming tools to suck the oil from the water. Put the removed oil into the waste pan (the small foil pie pan).

3 Use a sorbent.

Spread a sorbent such as hay over the oil and then scoop it out with a plastic spoon. Or make a sorbent sack by cutting the foot section off a pair of pantyhose and then filling it with a sorbent such as kitty litter or sawdust. Tie the end of the hose to keep the sorbent inside. Drag the sorbent sack through the ocean to collect any remaining oil. Put the used sorbents into the waste pan.

4 If you choose to do so, use a dispersant.

Decide how you will break up the oil slick that remains and what you will do (if anything) with the oil.

As you carry out your clean-up plan, document what you do in words, sketches, and photos (if you like to take pictures). Keep track of how much material you use to complete each action in your plan. Write down the result of each action. Here are some questions you can ask yourself for each step in your process:

» How well did a material or process work in removing the oil?

» About how much of the spill did the material or process clean up?

» Did the material or process make the oil spill easier or harder to clean up?

» Did the material or process cause the oil to move deeper in the water?

» How long did it take to complete a process?

» Would you repeat that process to remove more oil?

EVALUATE YOUR SUCCESS

Engineers must evaluate their work to decide whether they are successful in completing a job. The notes and pictures you record of your clean-up process will help you measure how well your process worked. In this project, you can decide

whether you were able to clean the water enough to consider it safe.

Because this is a simulation, it may be hard to know whether the water is really clean. Set a target to decide. For example, your target might be the following: "If I scoop up half a cup of water from five places in the ocean and it contains only one drop or no drops of oil, the water is cleaner." Or, "If I can reduce the liquid layer to just a thin rainbow-colored sheen on the surface, the water is cleaner." Try it!

IMPROVE YOUR PROCESS

Practice makes perfect. The experience you get from cleaning up one oil spill will help you improve when cleaning up future oil spills. In this phase of the Engineering Cycle, you learn from this project and find ways of repeating your successes and avoiding any failures.

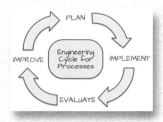

Look at the evaluation notes you made of your clean-up process and perform these steps:

1 **For a material or a process that worked well, circle it and put a star next to it.**

Note that this is something you should repeat!

2 **For a material or a process that sort of worked, underline it and note how it was partly successful. Also write down how you would try to improve it next time.**

3 **For a material or a process that failed, place an X through it and note why you don't recommend repeating it.**

NEW TRENDS IN OIL SPILL CLEAN UP

A research team Case Western Reserve University has invented a new, lightweight aerogel sponge to soak up ocean oil spills. The oil can then be recycled!

Another research team, this one from the University of Bristol, has made a soap that becomes magnetic when it is placed in water. The soap clings to the oil, and then the soap and oil can both be pulled to the ocean's surface — and removed! — by using magnets.

The work you perform will also be helpful when telling other junior engineers the best ways to clean up an oil spill if this is a job they will have to do.

IRON TRIANGLE OF ENGINEERING

Your last step in wrapping up your ocean oil spill project is to decide how this project is like cleaning up an oil spill in the real world. In a real-world spill, the Iron Triangle of Engineering would tell us that we can usually do only two out of 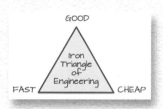 the following three things: a good clean-up job, a fast clean-up job, and a cheap clean-up job.

Which two would you pick and why? If you made your living on a fishing boat in the water where the spill occurred, which two would matter most to you? If you own the company that caused the spill and has to pay to clean it up, which two would matter most to you?

 Now that you're a clean-up expert, don't forget to clean up your work area by wrapping all used materials in newspapers and disposing of them properly. You can pour the remaining ocean water down the sink because the simulated oil spill is made with canola oil. Wash your hands and put everything away before removing your goggles.

MINI PROJECT
CLEANING FEATHERS AND FUR

IN THIS MINI PROJECT, YOU'LL CLEAN OCEAN ANIMALS CAUGHT IN AN OIL SPILL. What chemical best cleans oil from feathers and fur?

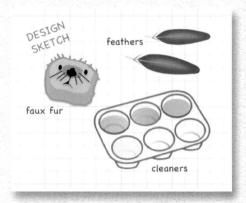

DESIGN SKETCH

feathers

faux fur

cleaners

Materials: Faux feathers and fur; water; cupcake pan; disposable foil roasting pan; disposable cup; plastic spoon; sponge; water; goggles; protective gloves and mask.

Materials to be supervised: Canola oil (1/2 cup); oil-based food coloring (red); safe cleaners (such as liquid soap, witch hazel, red wine vinegar, lemon juice).

Design: In your design notebook, sketch the layout of chemicals.

Warning: Wear safety equipment when working with chemicals!

Implement: Create the simulated oil in a disposable cup (see the "Simulate the Oil Spill" section). Coat a feather or piece of fur in the oil and then place it in the pie pan. Pour a different cleaner into each opening in the cupcake pan. Dip a sponge in one of the cleaners, and then work to remove the oil from the feather or fur, rinsing occassionally with water. After cleaning one simulated oiled animal, repeat the process with another oiled feather or fur and a different cleaner.

Evaluate: Is the feather or fur damaged by the cleaning process? How well does each cleaner remove the oil? How long does the cleaning process take?

Tip: Environmental engineers use Dawn dish soap to clean oiled animals!

PROJECT 5 LOAD THE BRIDGE

AGING CITY STRUCTURES – PIPES, ROADS, AND BRIDGES – ARE A MAJOR PROBLEM. As materials wear down, structures collapse and lives are at risk. The collapse of the Mississippi River Bridge was a shocking reminder that nothing lasts forever.

But as a junior engineer, you can do your part to build a strong, stable bridge that supports the load of passing cars and stands the test of time. You start by modeling a virtual bridge. Then you design and construct a pasta bridge by firing up your hot-glue gun and assembling penne, lasagna, spaghetti and pipe cleaners to meet certain design specifications. Finally, you load test your bridge to determine how much mass it can hold before failing. It's a real-world challenge. Are you up to the task? Yes!

Courtesy of tupungato/Getty

CIVIL ENGINEERS BUILD THE WORLD

The people who build the connection between humans and the natural world are called *civil engineers* — they design the physical part of civilization. Some of the structures they create are easy to see, such as bridges, roads, and dams. Civil engineers also work on a part of the city you almost never see, such as water pipes, sewage, gas, electricity, and telecommunications lines. Together, all the structures that build a city are called *infrastructure*.

INTRODUCTION TO BRIDGES

A bridge is a structure that lets you to cross a river or a road, while still letting you travel below. Traveling above a small river may be easy if you can fill the *span* (the gap) with a sturdy log (see Project 3). The log needs support only at the two ends, on each riverbank. But larger gaps are hard to span without more supports.

A wide variety of bridges exist, but the *truss bridge* is one of the most popular bridges. This type of bridge 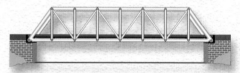 is made of triangle shapes. The beams in the triangles can stay strong during *tension* (pulling) and *compression* (pushing). The activities in this project focus on truss bridges.

OTHER TYPES OF BRIDGES

Many different bridge types have been designed and built to meet different design specifications. The most common types follow.

A *beam bridge* is a simple span of beams with *abutments* (end supports).

An *arch bridge* has a natural shape that carries the load along the curve of the arch to the piers.

A *cantilever bridge* is made of "diving board" shapes, with a beam connecting the free ends of each pair.

In a *cable-stayed bridge*, cables attached in fan shapes at the tops of the towers pull up to support the deck load.

A *suspension bridge* has a long cable that is strung across the tops of the towers. *Vertical* (up and down) cables attach the long cable to the deck — the vertical cables pull up to support the deck.

MATERIALS

Gather the following materials to conduct your project:

» Protective gear: goggles; protective gloves (optional for use while hot-gluing)

» Computer with Internet connection

» Bridge deck: lasagna (1 box)

» Truss structure: pipe cleaners (20); penne pasta (2 boxes)

» Cross-bracing: spaghetti (1 box)

» Traffic: Hot Wheels or other small cars (8)

» Low-temperature hot-glue gun and glue sticks (10)

» Meter stick, measuring tape, or ruler

» Scissors

» Kitchen scale

» Load test materials: dog leash or rope; large bucket or tub; cans of soda (24 to 48); two tables or desks (same height)

MODEL YOUR BRIDGE WITH TECHNOLOGY

A *simulation* helps you learn how to design a bridge before you actually construct it. One helpful and fun simulation is Cargo Bridge at the Coolmath Games website: www.coolmath-games.com/0-cargo-bridge.

Create a virtual bridge as follows:

1 On the Welcome to Cargo Bridge screen, click Start Game.

The Select Level page appears.

2 Click the Level 1 button.

Or click a different button if you have previously leveled up.

The Level 1 page appears.

3 View the design challenge and your bank balance ($500).

4 Click the Design Your Bridge icon, in the upper-left corner.

The icon looks like a ruler and a triangle. The Level 1 Bridge Design page appears.

5 Select the Wood walk material, on the right side of the page.

6 As shown in the figure, click a circle-shaped *joint* (a place where members connect) and then drag out a *member* (a beam).

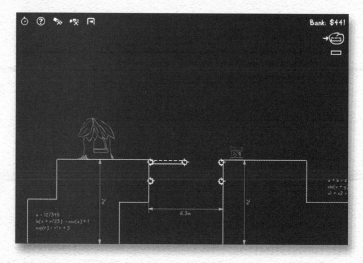

Release your mouse when the member is the length you want. The member will appear with a joint at the end. (Note: If the member is too long, it will turn red and you will see the following message: "The connector is too long.") The cost of the beam you built appears, and is subtracted from the bank.

7 Click the joint where you left off in Step 6, and draw a new member to connect the first beam to the joint at the wall.

8 Select the Wood connector material on the right side of the page.

9 As shown in the figure, click a joint and draw a diagonal member to connect to the Wood walk center joint. Click the joint where you left off and draw another diagonal member to connect to the joint at the wall.

To delete a member, select the member and press the Delete Selected icon in the upper-left corner. The member is removed and the cost is returned to your bank balance.

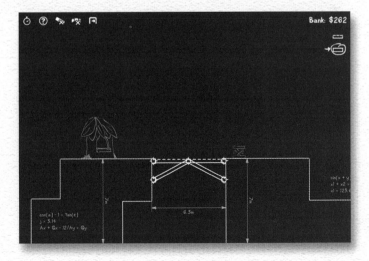

Note that you have created triangle shapes with the members and joints of the bridge. Bridges built with triangles are truss bridges.

If you run out of money, you will need to clear your project and start over. Click the Clear Project icon in the upper-left corner to do so. The members are removed and your starting bank balance is restored.

10 **Press the Test Your Bridge icon (stopwatch) in the upper-left corner.**

If your bridge succeeds, you receive a "You Have Won!" message and can click the Next Level button to move to the next level in the bridge design challenge.

Another option is to replay the level and try to rebuild at the lowest possible cost.

11 **If your bridge fails, as shown here on Level 3, click the Design Your Bridge icon and then the Clear Project icon — and then redesign your bridge.**

DESIGN YOUR TRUSS BRIDGE

After building and testing truss bridges with the Cargo Bridge simulation, you will be ready to design, construct, and test a pasta bridge. To be successful, every bridge must address many design *criteria* (standards for doing something). These include

» **Span:** The length of the bridge to fill the gap.

» **Clearance:** The height of objects that can go under the bridge.

» **Deck:** The surface where people or cars cross the bridge.

» **Load (live load):** How much mass the bridge supports. (What is heaviest that all the cars, boats, and people crossing the bridge can be?)

» **Mass (dead load):** The mass of the bridge itself. (How heavy are the joints and members that make the bridge?)

» **Supports:** The parts that connect the bridge to the ground below. *Abutments* are end supports; *piers* are supports in-between. The number needed depends on other criteria.

» **Environment:** The weather and geography where the bridge will be built. Wind, rough waters, hot or cold temperatures, or earthquake zones can damage a bridge.

» **Aesthetics:** The style and overall beauty of the structure, which may be a landmark in a community.

MORE BRIDGE DESIGNER SOFTWARE

For junior engineers seeking more complex — but still fun — bridge design software, Engineering Encounters offers a free tool called Bridge Designer. This software allows you to design a variety of bridge types, using different materials and member sizes; it also tracks bridge cost as you design. When you simulate bridge function, each member is color-coded to indicate whether it is in tension or compression. Software versions for both Macintosh and Windows are available at https://bridgecontest.org/.

In this project, you can set any design criteria you want. So let's set just a few criteria: a span that is long enough for four Hot Wheels cars to drive over, bumper to bumper; a deck that is wide enough for two lanes of Hot Wheels cars to pass each other; and no piers. Build the bridge to support the heaviest load you can while not breaking the bank on construction materials.

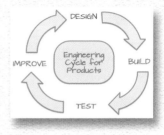

During the design phase of the Engineering Cycle, sketch the design of your truss bridge. Be sure your product meets your design criteria. The truss bridge you draw should be your own idea — use this example as a starting point, but feel free to create any bridge design you want.

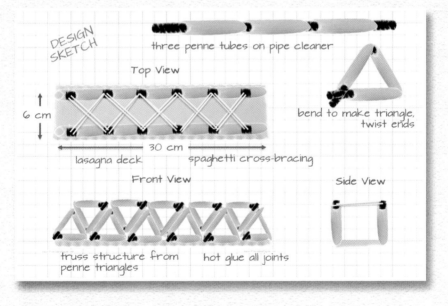

Make a few sketches, adding more specific details in your final design. Include in your final sketch the materials and dimensions you will use when you build your bridge — for example, a deck made of lasagna with a span length of 30 cm and a width of 6 cm.

Design criteria *describe the engineering problem to be solved. Details about exactly how to meet those criteria (including materials and dimensions) are* specifications.

BUILD YOUR PASTA BRIDGE

Gather the materials and tools you'll need to build your pasta bridge. Protect your eyes by wearing goggles during the building process, especially when cutting pipe cleaners and working with hot glue. Heat up the hot-glue gun and then follow the building procedures in

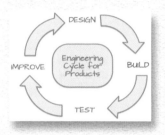

this section. Adjust the steps to match the design plans you have created.

1 Construct truss triangles.

Thread three penne pasta tubes onto a pipe cleaner. Bend the penne into a triangle, keeping the joints as tight as possible. Twist the ends of the pipe cleaner to lock in the triangle shape. Trim the ends of the pipe cleaner. Create 15 triangles. (You can always make more later, if needed.)

2 Build the deck.

Lay a lasagna noodle on the table. The length should be about 30 cm — it should already meet design specifications. Working quickly, eject several strips of hot glue along the length of the noodle. Place a second lasagna noodle on top and gently squeeze the two noodles together. Don't break them! You may choose to repeat the process to create a third layer of deck. This adds additional support to the bridge but increases its mass.

3 Build one truss (one side of the bridge).

On the table, line up truss triangles as shown. Hot-glue the joints. Continue adding triangles until the length of the truss matches the length of the deck.

4 Repeat Step 3 to build the other truss.

5 Attach the trusses to the deck.

Hot-glue the base of one truss to the long edge of the deck. When the glue has dried, repeat to attach the second truss to the other side.

6 Create cross braces.

Snap off lengths of spaghetti and hot-glue them across the bridge, connecting diagonal joints at the tops of the trusses. Each cross brace should form the shape of an X when viewed from the top. Cross bracing gives extra support to the trusses and keeps them from falling over.

As a final step, check your bridge to ensure that it is stable and you have no loose joints or broken members. If you do, use a little bit of hot glue to repair them. Then unplug the hot-glue gun and put it in a safe place to cool off.

Your finished bridge may look similar or very different from the example shown here! Thousands of variations are possible, even among truss bridges. Be sure to photograph your bridge before moving on to the next step, where you load test it to the point of failure!

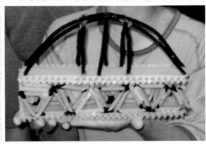

TEST YOUR PASTA BRIDGE

The test phase of the Engineering Cycle for Products is where you test the product you have designed and built. Here, you measure the mass of the bridge and then load test it to find out how much mass it can support.

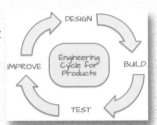

1 **Use a kitchen scale to measure the mass of the bridge.**

The number will be in grams. Write this number in your design notebook.

2 **Place two tables or desks close to each other, with a gap between them.**

The gap should be slightly smaller than the span of your bridge.

3 **Position your bridge so that it spans the gap between the tables.**

Each end of the bridge will be supported by a table. The tables serve as abutments.

4 **Use a kitchen scale to measure the mass of the dog leash or rope.**

Write this number in your design notebook.

5 Thread the leash or rope through your bridge.

The leash should be threaded through the center, resting flat on the deck, with equal lengths of the leash hanging down off the bridge, between the tables.

6 Use a kitchen scale to measure the mass of the bucket.

Write this number in your design notebook.

7 Attach the ends of the leash to the bucket.

Make sure the bucket is not resting on the ground. The figure shows the side view of the bridge, leash, and bucket.

8 Begin loading cans of soda, one at a time, into the bucket.

Pause for a few seconds before adding the next can. Count how many cans the bridge can support before it fails — cracks or breaks completely. Write this number in your notebook.

9 Compute the strength of the bridge.

The strength is the total load the bridge supports, including the bridge itself:

strength (g) = bridge + leash + bucket + cans (all in grams)

Each can of soda has a mass of about 385 grams (15 grams for the can and 370 grams for the soda).

10 **Compute the strength-to-mass ratio of the bridge:**

strength (g) / mass of bridge (g)

The larger this ratio, the better! It means the bridge is strong for its mass.

When measuring mass, it might help to know that the mass of a paperclip is about one gram (1g) and the mass of three full soda cans is about one kilogram (1 kg).

IMPROVE YOUR BRIDGE

The improve phase of the Engineering Cycle is a time to rethink your product design and make changes to improve how it performs when tested.

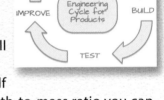

Because you test a bridge to failure, you'll have to build a new bridge after making design improvements. Challenge yourself to build a bridge with the highest strength-to-mass ratio you can achieve!

CIVIL ENGINEERING AND THE IRON TRIANGLE

The Iron Triangle of Engineering tells us that we can do only two of the following three things: a good job, as fast as you can, for cheap. When building a bridge, or constructing any civil engineering project, you must always do a good job because lives are at stake.

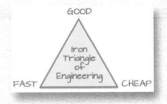

Many emergencies, such as building flood control structures or roads, require you to get the job done fast. This may be true when building a bridge if there are no other ways to span a gap where people must travel. Budgets may demand that you complete a civil engineering project for as low a cost as possible. This is because tax dollars usually pay for civil engineering projects, and governments require these costs to be as low as possible. How would you balance good, fast, and cheap on a civil engineering project such as building a bridge?

BIOMIMICRY: NATURE-INSPIRED ENGINEERING

Floods cause bridge failure more often than fire, wind, earthquakes, overloading, aging, and crashes combined! Engineers measure how flood waters make the river bottom less stable, which weakens the bridge foundation. At the same time, they look at nature to find a solution by *mimicking* (copying) a fish that swims in the same areas — the salmon!

Salmon have hairlike sensors on their bodies that send information about the direction and speed of water flowing around them. By building this same type of sensor on bendable copper rods and then attaching them to bridge supports, changes in the sediments can be tracked during a flood. Turning to nature for ways to engineer our world is called *biomimicry.*

(continued)

(continued)

Courtesy of asxsoonxas/Getty

Courtesy of chuyu/Getty

Another area of civil engineering that has used biomimicry in its design is transportation. In Japan, bullet trains were reaching such high speeds that big pressure waves were created at the front of trains moving through tunnels. This required more fuel to push the train forward, and caused a loud boom each time a train exited a tunnel.

An engineer noticed that the kingfisher bird, with its long pointy beak, can dive at high speeds into the water with no splash. The front of the train was then reengineered to mimic the kingfisher beak. With the nose of the train longer and pointier, it cuts through the air more smoothly, making less sound and using less fuel.

Nature has tried billions of designs during Earth's existence, and only the best ones that have stood the test of time are still around — why not mimic them in our engineering designs?

PROJECT 6 ELECTRIC ALIEN CAP

MANY SCHOOLS CELEBRATE SPIRIT WEEK: A TIME OF FUN, CHEER, AND CRAZY COSTUMES. Making your own award-winning, crazy hat is a snap with the help of a little *DIY* (do-it-yourself) engineering. In this project, you use basic concepts of electrical engineering to construct a cool baseball cap. The cap will have glowing LED lights wired in a circuit using a LilyTwinkle board and conductive thread.

You can also choose to explore simple 3D design and printing to make more decorations for your cap. The design in this project features an alien head with glimmering eyes, pointy ears, and springy antennae, but yours can capture any character or theme you can image. Remember, the crazier, the better!

Courtesy dubassy/Shutterstock

ELECTRONICS 101

You know the zap you feel when you shuffle your feet across the carpet and then touch a doorknob? That's *static electricity* — a quick flow of charged particles called *electrons*. Now imagine that zap flowing constantly! *Electricity* results from the flow of electric charge.

You probably use electrical energy most often by plugging something into a wall outlet. The electricity you receive starts in a giant facility that produces power from fossil fuels, nuclear, or green sources (see Project 7). Electrical engineers build a system that sends power from that facility to thousands of buildings and millions of outlets. That system makes it possible for you to run the air conditioning, lights, and television in your home.

Courtesy of saemilee/Getty

ELECTRICAL CIRCUITS

For mobile devices, such as your cellphone or an electric car, a *battery* is needed to store and supply electricity so that it is available on the go. The battery is just one *component* (part) in the electrical circuit that forms the device. The *electrical circuit* is like a map that routes electricity through tiny wires to the components that need energy to run, such as lights, speakers, and motors. The electricity keeps looping around the circuit, keeping things on, until the battery dies or a switch is opened, stopping the flow.

SYMBOLS AND SCHEMATICS

A *schematic diagram* is a drawing that shows how to build an electrical circuit. It's like a blueprint that an architect draws to build a house. The schematic shows a special symbol for each component in the circuit. Here are symbols for a battery, a switch for turning the circuit off and on, and a light bulb.

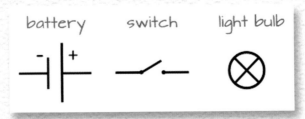

Here is a schematic showing the battery, switch, and light bulb all connected in a circuit. Electricity flows from the positive (+) side of the battery around the loop to the negative (−) side. The negative side is called *ground*. The wires connecting the components are shown in gold. Next to the schematic is a computer simulation showing a model of the circuit. The switch is closed and the electricity is flowing to the light bulb, which lights up!

You can tinker with this computer simulation to build your own circuits. Just download the simulation from https://phet.colorado.edu/en/simulation/circuit-construction-kit-dc.

SERIES AND PARALLEL CIRCUITS

Lighting one light bulb is fun, but lighting two bulbs is twice as much fun! You can light up two light bulbs in a circuit by connecting the bulbs in series or in parallel.

A *series circuit* sends electricity through the components one after another. It's easy to wire: Put the components in a circle and connect the positive side of one component to the ground side of the next component. In a series circuit, if one component burns out, electricity stops flowing and the circuit stops working. Here is a schematic and a simulation of two light bulbs in series.

A *parallel circuit* sends electricity through all components at the same time. This type of circuit requires more wiring: You connect the positive side of all the components to each other, then connect that to the positive side of the battery; connect the ground side of all the components to each other, then connect that to the ground side of the battery. In a parallel circuit, if one component burns out, electricity still flows through the other components — the circuit still works. Here is a schematic and a simulation of two light bulbs in parallel:

Light bulbs in a series circuit glow less brightly the more bulbs you add. Light bulbs in a parallel circuit glow the same as a single bulb — even if you add lots and lots of bulbs!

As you get ready to make your electric alien cap, you will need to know a few more schematic symbols. Here are symbols for an LED light, a *resistor,* which reduces the flow of electricity, and an *IC (integrated circuit),* which is a component with lots of different parts built into it that do complicated functions. In this project, you use an IC on a board called a *LilyTwinkle.* When connected in a circuit with LED lights, the LilyTwinkle slowly changes the brightness of the lights.

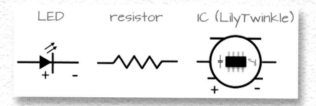

The LilyTwinkle board has both an integrated circuit and a capacitor. *The capacitor temporarily stores and then releases some electricity. Together, the IC and the capacitor make the LEDs twinkle.*

MATERIALS

The example shown in this project is an electric alien cap. But you can use any clothing item to create your spirit wear! Do you want to make a crazy T-shirt, a fun hat, or silly socks? Go for it! If you are making the same cap I show here, use these materials:

» Protective gear: goggles; protective gloves (optional for use while hot-gluing)

» ProtoSnap LilyTwinkle (available from www.sparkfun.com); the all-in-one kit includes a LilyTwinkle, a LilyPad coin cell battery holder with switch, a coin cell battery, LilyPad white LEDs (4), stainless steel conductive thread (10 m), a needle set

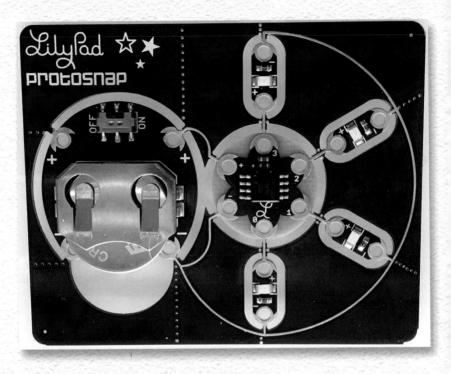

» Baseball cap: black, soft

» Antennae: pipe cleaners (2)

» Felt square: neon pink, thin (approximately 6 cm by 6 cm)

» Ears: 3D printed ears (optional)

» Hot-glue gun and glue sticks

» Thin white chalk or metallic marker

» Scissors

DESIGN YOUR ELECTRIC ALIEN CAP

As always, begin the Engineering Cycle for Products with the design phase.

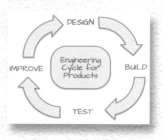

For my project, I designed a black baseball cap with a pink alien head, glowing white eyes, fuzzy antennae, and green plastic ears. My design sketches show a few different things: my finished cap; my schematic for the circuit I will stitch; and where I will sew stitches and components onto the cap.

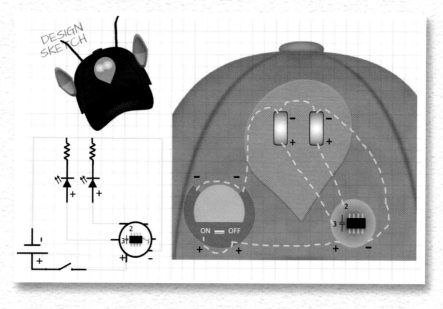

Here are some things to keep in mind about the schematic and the actual process of building the circuit for the cap:

» The battery and the switch are on a single component.

» This design is using a parallel circuit.

» Each LED component has a resistor already built in.

» The design shows the components and stitches on the outside of the hat. This is the easiest way to build a design when you are first getting started. More experienced readers can sew the battery and LilyTwinkle onto the inside of the cap.

» The kit comes with four LEDs, but this project uses only two. One LED is connected to pin 2 on the LilyTwinkle board, and the other LED is connected to pin 3. Although I use the term "pin," you will actually stitch through a hole on the board.

You can use all four LEDs in your design, but you will need to redesign your circuit so that is uses all four pins (0, 1, 2, and 3) on the LilyTwinkle.

BUILD YOUR CAP

Gather your materials and get to work building your electrical engineering product. The electronics components are small, so work in a well-lit area so you can see what you are doing. Protect your eyes by wearing goggles during the building process, especially when sewing, cutting pipe cleaners, and working with hot glue.

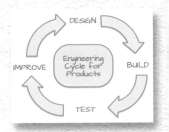

GET YOUR COMPONENTS READY

Carefully press the components out of the ProtoSnap frame. Remember, you need only two LED lights. Thread the needle with about 50 cm of conductive thread. Make sure an equal length (about 25 cm) is hanging down on each side of the eye of the needle. Tie the ends of the thread (note that your thread is now double in thickness). Arrange your components as shown. The thread will both secure the parts onto the cap and connect them electrically.

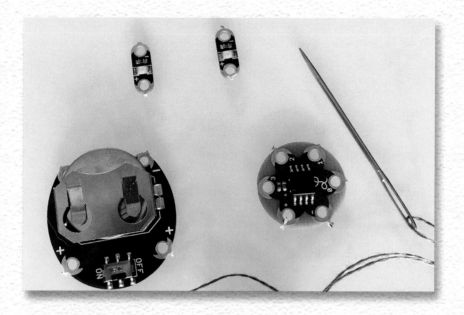

MARK YOUR CIRCUIT ONTO THE HAT

Use a sharp piece of chalk or metallic marker to mark your planned circuit onto your cap. Also mark the outline of where you plan to put the alien head.

The wires are conductive thread — they contain metal. When sewing your circuit, don't cross the wires!

STITCH THE POSITIVE CONNECTIONS IN YOUR CIRCUIT

Follow these steps to attach your circuit to the cap:

1 **Sew down the positive (+) side of the battery holder.**

Position the battery holder on the cap. (The battery should not be in the holder at this point.) Stitch three loops securing the positive (+) hole

near the On side of the switch to hold down the battery holder. Continue stitching a simple in-and-out line along the cap, around the curve, below the switch. Then stitch three loops through the + hole near the Off side of the switch. The battery holder should now be secure.

2 **Connect the positive (+) side of the battery holder to the positive hole of the LilyTwinkle board.**

Continuing where you left off, stitch a line across the cap until you reach the place where you will put the LilyTwinkle board. Position the LilyTwinkle on the cap and stitch through the positive (+) hole of the LilyTwinkle. Stitch a total of three loops through the + hole to secure the LilyTwinkle.

Direction matters — double-check which holes you are connecting with your stitches. Remember, positive (+) connects to positive. Ground (–) connects to ground.

3 **Tie off and cut the thread.**

4 **Thread the needle with another length of conductive thread (double thickness) and tie the end.**

5 **Sew down pin 3 on the LilyTwinkle.**

Stitch three loops securing the hole at pin 3.

6 **Connect pin 3 on the LilyTwinkle to the positive (+) hole on the first LED.**

Stitch the line across the cap. Position the LED at the end point.

Double-check the direction of your LEDs. If you reverse the direction of an LED in a circuit, it will not light.

7 **Stitch three loops through the + hole on the LED.**

8 **Tie off and cut the thread.**

9 **Thread the needle with another length of conductive thread (double thickness) and tie the end.**

10 **Sew down pin 2 on the LilyTwinkle.**

Stitch three loops securing the hole at pin 2.

11 **Connect pin 2 on the LilyTwinkle to the positive (+) hole on the second LED.**

Stitch the line across the cap. Position the LED at the end point.

12 **Stitch three loops to secure the positive (+) hole on the second LED.**

13 **Tie off and cut the thread.**

STITCH THE GROUND CONNECTIONS IN YOUR CIRCUIT

Follow these steps to complete and close your circuit:

1 **Thread the needle with another length of conductive thread (double thickness) and tie the end.**

Make this length a little longer, around 70 cm, so that you can complete all the ground connections with one piece of thread.

2 **Sew down the ground (–) side of the battery holder.**

Stitch three loops securing the ground (–) hole on the side close to the On switch. Continue stitching on the cap around the curve to the second – hole on the battery holder. Stitch three loops securing this hole.

3 **Connect the ground (–) side of the battery holder to the ground hole of the first LED.**

Continuing where you left off, stitch a line across the cap until you reach the first LED. Stitch three loops securing the ground hole of this LED.

4 **Connect the ground (–) side of the first LED to the ground hole of the second LED.**

Continuing where you left off, stitch a line across the cap until you reach the second LED. Stitch three loops securing the ground hole of this LED.

5 **Connect the ground (–) side of the second LED to the ground hole of LilyTwinkle.**

Continuing where you left off, stitch a line across the cap until you reach the ground hole of the LilyTwinkle. Stitch three loops through the ground hole.

6 **Stitch three loops to secure the ground (–) hole of LilyTwinkle.**

7 **Tie off and cut the thread.**

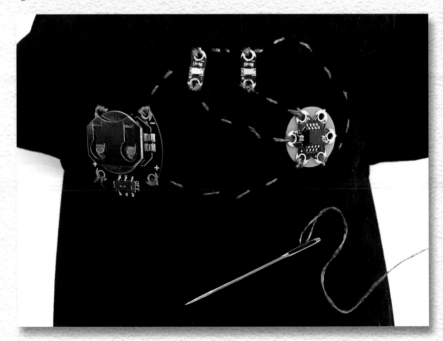

TEST YOUR CIRCUIT

The test phase of the Engineering Cycle for products is where you test the product you have designed and built. Place the battery in the battery holder. The larger flat side (the side with the writing) should be facing you. The battery should be firm and secure in the battery holder.

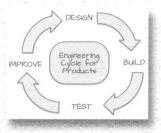

Turn the switch on and watch your alien eyes light up! If they don't, trace the wires you stitched and make sure they match your design diagrams. Common mistakes include crossing wires and turning the LED components in the wrong direction.

IMPROVE YOUR CAP

If your circuit works, you can improve your cap by adding extra decorations such as a felt alien head and antennae.

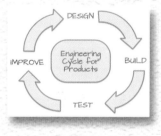

Cut an alien head from the felt. Hot-glue the felt on the cap, but avoid placing glue on any wire or component. Your battery, wires, and LilyTwinkle will still show — this is part of the cap's high-tech look! Stick antennae through the vent holes (the little circles) on the cap. Poke a pipe cleaner through each hole and then hot-glue the connection inside the cap.

ELECTRICAL ENGINEERING AND THE IRON TRIANGLE

The Iron Triangle of Engineering says we cannot do a good job, a fast job, and a cheap job all at the same time. Many products in our world rely on electronics, from mobile phones to traffic lights to

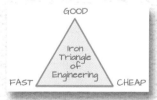

heart pacemakers. Which parts of the Iron Triangle do you think are most important when it comes to building electronics?

3D PRINTING ALIEN EARS

Aliens are known for their sparkly eyes and their wacky ears. Using a free, online program, you can design your own alien ears! Go to www.tinkercad.com, create an account, and begin designing. Tinkercad works like a drawing program, allowing you to create 3D solids instead of 2D pictures.

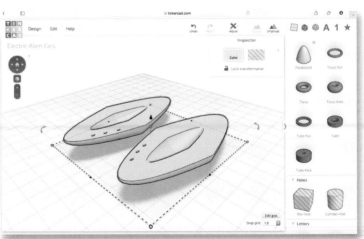

Tinkercad has a library of 3D shapes and holes that you can grow or shrink and then put together in different ways. The alien ears you see here are made from paraboloid solids with smaller paraboloid holes and large box holes (cutting off the front half of each shape). Once one ear is made, you can group the shapes and holes, and then copy and paste to make another ear. You can add holes to each ear for sewing the ears onto the cap (or you can just hot-glue the ears to your cap). Finally, you can save and send the Tinkercad file to a 3D printer (such as the M3D) to print!

It may take some practice to get the hang of moving around in three dimensions, but you can improve your technique by watching Tinkercad tutorials at the Help menu and on YouTube. If you want to use the Electric Alien Ears shown here, just search for them in the Tinkercad Collections!

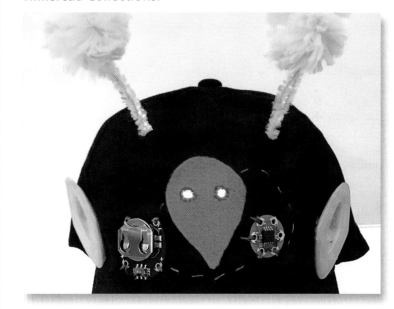

PROJECT 7 NOW YOU'RE COOKING!

MECHANICAL ENGINEERS DESIGN AND BUILD MACHINES AND SYSTEMS. Pumps, pulleys, robots, refrigerators, cars, and cookers were all developed by mechanical engineers. Machines need energy to run, and that energy can come in many different forms.

This project invites you to explore *thermodynamics* — how energy does work and changes into different forms. You'll focus on heat energy, as you construct a *solar* (sun energy) cooker to harness the power of the sun. Using everyday materials, you'll direct and trap energy in an "eco-bake oven" to heat up an afternoon snack!

Courtesy of bhofack2/Getty

EARLY MECHANICAL ENGINEERING

The very first mechanical engineer was probably the inventor of the wheel — a machine used as a potter's wheel long before it made chariots mobile! Much later, in the third century BCE, a

Greek inventor named Archimedes engineered many products and processes that we still use today.

ARCHIMEDES THE ENGINEER

One of Archimedes's key inventions was a process for measuring the volume of an irregular shape, such as a crown, to test whether the shape's material was pure or fake. A popular story is that Archimedes brainstormed his method based on the way that the water rose as he got into the bathtub.

Courtesy of bilhagolan/Getty

As a mechanical engineer, Archimedes is also famous for inventing products, such as the Archimedes Screw. This machine — which looks like a screw inside a tube — is used to move materials and fluids. The Archimedes Screw was designed to move water uphill to irrigate land. (See the sidebar at the end

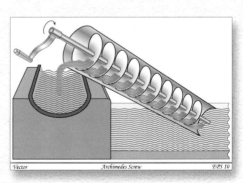

Courtesy of Fouad A. Saad/Shutterstock

of this project for additional information on the screw and other simple machines in mechanical engineering.)

Archimedes is especially famous for a "death ray" machine that reflected sunlight off mirrors, probably bronze shields, to burn attacking ships. The Mythbusters crew re-created this engineering marvel and found that it most likely caused a singe, not an explosion of flames. But it shows the power of combining the sun and reflective surfaces to make a hot spot.

Courtesy of Giulio Parigi, public domain

ENERGY EVERYWHERE

Understanding different forms of energy and how they can be used to make machines operate is a key job of the mechanical engineer. Many forms of energy exists; here are just a few and how they are used:

» **Biochemical energy:** The fuel your body converts from food that then allows you to move, play, and think.

» **Electrical energy:** Electricity that runs the devices "plugged in" inside your house.

» **Green energy:** Energy that is supplied by nature, such as sunlight, ocean waves, geothermal, and wind, and others.

» **Light energy:** Energy from *photons* (light particles) that beam from a flashlight or a laser.

» **Mechanical energy:** The energy of an object from its motion and position, such as the energy of a roller coaster going up and down during a ride. (See Project 8.)

» **Thermal energy:** Heat energy, used for processes such as cooking food; also comes from friction between surfaces.

THE FIRST LAW OF THERMODYNAMICS

The *First Law of Thermodynamics* states that energy can be transferred from one form to another, but you can't create it and you can't destroy it. For example, chemical energy from a battery becomes electrical energy that causes an LED to shine, giving off light energy (see Project 6). Radiant energy from the sun, a form of green energy, becomes the thermal energy that warms food in a solar cooker.

MATERIALS

Archimedes probably never imagined that his death ray design could be reworked to cook snacks with thermal energy. But like all good mechanical engineers, Archimedes observed his world, saw problems that needed solutions, and then worked to design and build those solutions. Now it's your turn to continue that work!

To conduct this project, you will need:

» Protective gear: goggles for building and sunglasses for testing

» Structure: two boxes; one box fits inside the other with a few centimeters of gap between the boxes (approximately shoe box and boot box in size)

» Meter stick, measuring tape, or ruler

» Reflective material: foil, silver Mylar, mirror-silver cardstock, or a rectangular mirror (2 square meters)

» Heat-absorbing material: black construction paper, black butcher paper, black felt, or black cloth (2 square meters)

» Insulation: Styrofoam, cork, paper, wool, or felt (enough to fill the gap between the boxes)

» Cooking surface: dark, rectangular baking pan (to fit inside the small box)

» Adhesives: silver foil tape, clear tape, masking tape, and black electrical tape

» Window: plastic wrap or glass rectangle (from picture frame)

» Dowel rod (about 25 cm long)

» Scissors

» Thermometer

» Food ingredients: cheese and chips (for nachos); franks and buns (for hog dogs); or marshmallows, chocolate bars, and graham crackers (for s'mores)

Avoid using black trash bags inside your oven because they will melt at hot oven temperatures.

DESIGN YOUR SOLAR OVEN

In remote areas of the world, electricity is not available — but the natural power of sunlight is everywhere. That's why people in these regions build *solar ovens,* devices that cook using *thermal energy* (heat) from the sun. With the right materials, the sun's free energy, and good engineering design, you can construct an oven that heats a yummy meal. For people living in areas without clean drinking water, a solar oven can boil water to kill bacteria and make it *potable* (safe to drink).

THE SECOND LAW OF THERMODYNAMICS

A solar oven relies on the sun's rays to supply thermal energy. You can design the solar oven in many ways to collect the sun's energy. Like all mechanical engineering products, solar ovens must obey the *Second Law of Thermodynamics,* which says that heat flows from a hotter body to a colder one. This means heat flows from your oven to the colder food you are cooking. But it also means heat flows from the oven into its cooler outside surroundings.

OVEN DESIGN CRITERIA

Keeping this information in mind, your solar oven should address four design *criteria* (standards for doing something). Your oven should

» **Direct heat:** Use flat, shiny surfaces to reflect the sun's rays towards your oven. This heating method is called *radiation.*

» **Attract and absorb heat:** Coat the inside surfaces of the oven with dark colors, which absorb (soak up) heat from the sun's rays better than light colors.

» **Trap hot air:** Seal the oven tightly to trap the heated air inside the oven and prevent it from leaking out.

» **Be insulated:** To reduce heat loss, place materials around the oven that have low *conductivity values* — heat will not flow well through them.

During the design phase of the Engineering Cycle for Products, be sure your product meets these design criteria.

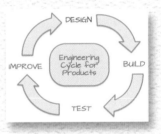

Sketch a few designs, adding more specific details in your final design. Include in your final sketch the materials and dimensions you will use when you build your oven.

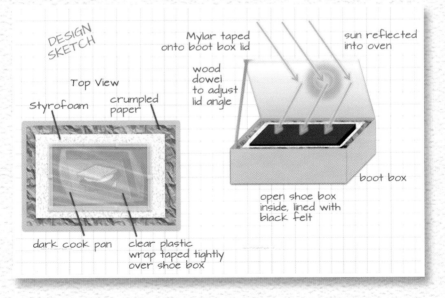

DESIGN SKETCH

Top View

Styrofoam

crumpled paper

Mylar taped onto boot box lid

wood dowel to adjust lid angle

sun reflected into oven

boot box

open shoe box inside, lined with black felt

dark cook pan

clear plastic wrap taped tightly over shoe box

Your design sketch may look very different from the example shown here, or it may look similar! The oven you draw should show your own best ideas — there is more than one way to design a solar oven.

BUILD YOUR DESIGN

Using your design sketch, gather the materials and tools you will need. Wear goggles to protect your eyes before you begin building your solar oven. Follow the general building procedure outlined here, adjusting the steps to match your design.

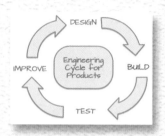

BUILD THE FOOD CHAMBER

The food chamber is the place where you will put your ingredients. Build your food chamber as follows:

1 **Remove the lid from the shoebox.**

The empty shoebox will be the food chamber. The shoebox lid will not be used, so set it aside.

2 **Measure and cut black felt to fit the inside walls and floor of the food chamber.**

3 **Using the black electrical tape, carefully attach the felt to cover the inside of the chamber.**

The dark color will attract and hold heat from the sun.

4 **Measure and cut a section of clear plastic wrap to completely cover the chamber. Don't tape down the plastic wrap yet.**

Rays from the sun will enter the food chamber through this clear material.

ADD THE OVEN INSULATION

The food chamber will be surrounded by the exterior oven structure. The space between the food chamber and the exterior of the oven, including all four sides and the bottom of the oven, must be filled with insulation. This insulation reduces heat loss, the quantity of heat that transfers out of the cooker.

Follow these steps to insulate the oven:

1 **Remove the lid from the boot box.**

The empty boot box will be the structure of the oven. The boot box lid will be used to make the solar reflector, so set it aside but don't throw it out.

2 **Crumple up small handfuls of newspaper or butcher paper and cover the floor of the oven in a single layer, 1-2 cm thick.**

The layer will contain lots of air pockets — this is fine!

3 **Using the masking tape, gently tape down the paper insulation to the base of the oven.**

4 **Add a layer of Styrofoam over the newspaper, 1-2 cm thick.**

The layer doesn't need to touch the walls of the oven.

5 **Set the food chamber on top of the insulation on the floor of the oven.**

6 **Surround the food chamber with a layer of Styrofoam, 1-2 cm thick.**

7 **Using a few pieces of masking tape, attach the Styrofoam in place around the chamber.**

8 **Crumple up more small handfuls of paper and fill in the gaps between the Styrofoam and the boot box.**

Again, the layer will contain lots of air pockets.

K-VALUES

Materials have a property called *thermal conductivity*, which tells how well the material conducts heat. The k-value is a number that measures thermal conductivity. Metals conduct heat well, so they have high k-values. For example, the k-value of aluminum is 205, which tells us that aluminum is a good conductor. The lower the k-value, the worse the material is at conducting heat, so materials with low numbers are good insulators.

The units of k are strange, so most of the time, a k-value is written as just a number. Here are some k-values of materials you might use as insulators:

Air: 0.024	Paper: 0.05	Sawdust: 0.08
Cork: 0.07	Felt: 0.07	Solid Rock: 2 to 7
Cotton: 0.04	Sand: 0.71	Styrofoam: 0.033

The k-value tells you only about the property of the material. Adding more layers of an insulator will result in better insulation.

ATTACH THE SOLAR REFLECTOR

The oven needs one or more reflectors to direct sunlight to the food chamber. Some solar ovens use four reflectors — one on each side of the food chamber — to increase the quantity of directed sunlight. Other solar ovens use a continuous, curved reflector that surrounds the top of the food chamber.

The example design uses a single reflector that is shaped like a rectangular mirror:

1   Measure and cut a rectangle of silver Mylar film to cover the inside of the boot box lid.

You may prefer to use foil instead of Mylar.

2   Using the silver foil tape, smoothly tape down the edges of the Mylar film to the lid.

3   Cut the corner connections at one of the long edges of the lid to create a long flap.

4   Using masking tape on the back side of the reflector, attach the reflector flap to the oven.

The lid should be secure, but you should still be able to open and close it.

5   Wedge the wood dowel rod between the oven insulation and the reflector lid.

The rod will prop up the lid. Tilt the dowel to different angles to adjust the position of the reflector. See the design sketch for an example.

LAW OF REFLECTION

The *Law of Reflection* tells how light rays bounce off of a smooth reflective surface. It says, "angle in equals angle out." This means that the angle at which sunlight hits a mirror is the same as the angle at which it reflects back. Adjusting the angle of the mirror allows you to adjust the sun's angle in, so that the sun's angle out hits a target. Use the Law of Reflection to help position your reflector for maximum solar heating in your oven.

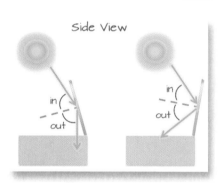

Side View

TEST YOUR DESIGN PLAN

Now it's time to test out your oven. Follow these steps:

1 Place your ingredients into a dark cooking pan.

2 Put the cooking pan inside the food chamber of your oven.

3 Cover the chamber with clear plastic wrap.

4 Pull the plastic tight and smooth, and then use clear tape to seal the edges around the food chamber.

5 Put on sunglasses, go outside midday, and place your oven in a sunny location.

6 Adjust the angle of the reflector to target the food chamber, and start cooking!

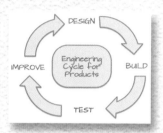

Your oven will probably take two to three times longer than a regular oven to cook your snack. Also, different food items will cook at different times.

If you want to measure the temperature of the food chamber, you can poke a traditional thermometer (or a digital thermometer with a probe) through the plastic wrap into the chamber. But if you do so, tape around the insertion point to prevent hot air from leaking out of the food chamber.

IMPROVE YOUR COOKER

When your snack has cooked, take it out and eat it! As you eat, think about how you will improve your oven in the future.

Will you adjust the size of your oven? Or use different insulation materials? Will you add additional reflectors to direct more of the sun's rays into the food chamber? Doing a *redesign* (a different design) of your product is an important job during the improve phase of the Engineering Cycle. The better your design, the better the food . . . now you're cooking!

SOLAR COOKING AND THE IRON TRIANGLE

The Iron Triangle of Engineering tells us that we can *maximize* (make the greatest) only two of the three goals when engineering a project: doing a good job, as fast as we can, for cheap.

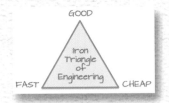

Around the world, solar cookers are popular because they are cheap to build (and operate) when compared with store-bought ovens. They can also be constructed fast because they require few materials, and the building process is easy. But a solar cooker may not be quite as good as a modern electric or gas oven due to the longer time it takes to cook a meal. Solar cookers may also not be able to reach the same high temperatures of modern ovens, and they do not function on cloudy days. Can you think of other ways to improve the good of your oven while still making it fast and cheap?

SIMPLE MACHINES AND ENERGY

Many designs in mechanical engineering, including some described by Archimedes, are based on simple machines. A simple machine is a device that changes the size or the direction of a force.

| Wedge | Wheel and Axle | Lever | Inclined Plane | Screw | Pulley |

Here are the six simple machines and an example of each:

» Wedge: an axe

» Wheel and axle: the wheel system on a wagon

» Lever: a see-saw

» Inclined plane: a wheelchair ramp

» Screw: an oil drill

» Pulley: a rope and wheel for raising a bucket of water from a well

Putting together these simple machines in different ways creates more complex machines. Every machine needs energy to operate, and the role of many machines is to change one type of energy into another. However, due to friction, some energy is always converted to heat or sound or other forms that the machine can't use to operate. Consult any introductory physics book for additional information on simple machines and energy.

MINI PROJECT
VDARA DEATH RAY

The *concave* (curving in) mirror face of the Las Vegas Vdara *converges* (brings together) solar rays near the pool. Model this engineering mistake — a hotel hot spot — that heated up guests and melted their plastic shopping bags!

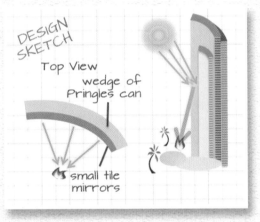

DESIGN SKETCH

Top View
wedge of Pringles can

small tile mirrors

Materials: Empty Pringles can; small mirror titles; plastic grocery bag; goggles and gloves (optional); sunglasses.

Materials to be supervised: Low-temp hot-glue gun and glue sticks; heavy-duty scissors.

Design: Sketch a scale model of the Vdara. At a scale of 1 cm = 10 m, the actual Vdara (178 m) will measure 18 cm tall. Model only the middle tower, which produces the hot spot (where all the sun's rays reflect to the same point — the *focal point*).

Build: Cut a quarter wedge from the Pringles can, about 18 cm tall. Hot-glue mirror tiles to cover the inside surface of the wedge.

Test: Put on your sunglasses and place your model Vdara in direct sunlight. Wad up a piece of plastic bag and place it at the focal point of the model. Does it heat up and melt?

Tip: Check out the real Vdara on Google Maps. The hotel added extra trees and umbrellas to the pool deck to protect guests — and their plastic shopping bags!

PROJECT *8* ROLLER COASTER MANIA

ROLLER COASTERS ARE FUN AND SCARY, BUT THEY ARE ALSO ENGINEERING WONDERS! Unlike other engineering fields, entertainment engineering is less focused on solving an urgent human or humanitarian need and more focused on creating exciting and fun experiences for its riders. Roller coasters are based on simple energy and motion ideas but become thrilling with an inventive design!

In this project, you use technology to build a model of a virtual coaster and simulate its ride. Then you'll use PVC pipes, foam tubing, masking tape, and a marble to create a crazy, functional roller coaster!

Courtesy of Michael Valdez/iStockphoto

INTRODUCTION TO ROLLER COASTERS

Some of the earliest roller coasters were carved out of hills of ice in what is now St. Petersburg. Called "Russian Mountains," the drops measured 25 meters and were supported by wooden beams. In 1884, at the Coney Island amusement park in New York, an American named LaMarcus Thompson engineered a more permanent (and probably warmer) roller coaster. Riders at Coney Island had to climb up to a deck to get on the roller coaster — which was basically a railroad car on a 200-meter stretch of tracks.

America's first roller coaster was called a switchback railway. After riders rode down the track, a railroad switch was used to move them to another track and return them to their starting point. The coaster moved at only six kilometers per hour and cost five cents to ride.

Thanks to modern engineering, roller coasters have come a long way from those early designs. If you've ever ridden a roller coaster, you know that the excitement of the ride comes from the drops, loops, twists, and changes in direction you feel as you speed along the track.

Entertainment engineers invent the wild track designs that make a roller coaster thrilling. They also select from a wide range of building materials to create a safe and reliable ride. Although wooden roller coasters are still around, many more coasters are built from steel. Roller coasters of the future may be made of even stronger, newly engineered materials.

A coaster may be designed for riding in a suspended position or on a track. A *track* coaster has cars that you sit in, surrounding your body, and are hooked to the track under your feet. A *suspended* roller coaster hangs from the track above your head so that your feet dangle free.

MASS IN A ROLLER COASTER SYSTEM

A roller coaster system is made up of cars that travel on the track. The number of cars in the coaster determines its mass. *Mass* is how much of something there is. More mass means more energy in the roller coaster system, and more energy means faster speeds. Less mass means less energy and slower speeds.

Mass can be measured in kilograms (kg). A bag of seven apples has a mass of about 1 kg.

ENERGY IN A ROLLER COASTER SYSTEM

A roller coaster system has three types of energy:

» **Potential energy (PE):** Stored energy. The coaster has the most potential energy at the start of the ride, when it is at its highest position in the ride.

» **Kinetic energy (KE):** The energy of motion. The coaster has a lot of kinetic energy when it is moving fast.

» **Dissipated energy (DE):** Heat and sound energy. When the coaster is in motion, there is friction (rubbing) between the cars and the track.

You must balance the three types of energy in your roller coaster system. The coaster goes back and forth between being high up in the air (high PE, low KE) and moving fast (low PE, high KE). The coaster dissipates energy (DE) while it is moving. It must change enough energy to sound and heat to slow down and come to a stop at the end of the ride.

MATERIALS

Gather the following materials to conduct your project:

» Protective gear: goggles

» Computer with Internet connection

» Coaster cart: marble or ball bearing (1 cm in diameter or similar)

» Track: gray insulation tubing (flexible foam) and PVC tubes and elbows (optional)

» Supports: string (a few feet), empty boxes or odd containers (varying sizes), wooden dowels of varying lengths (4 to 10)

» Masking tape or painter's tape

» Meter stick, measuring tape, or ruler

» Scissors

MODEL YOUR COASTER WITH TECHNOLOGY

A computer *simulation* is a digital model of something in the real world. A simulation can help you learn how to design a working roller coaster — before you use real tools and materials for the actual construction. You can learn how a coaster works, engineer possible layouts, test crazy ideas, and change your designs in the safety of the computer screen.

There are a lot of fun and helpful roller coaster simulations, but one of the best is the free JASON Digital Labs Coaster Creator at http://rollercoastergamesonline.com/roller-coaster-games/digital-labs-coaster-creator.

Create a virtual coaster as follows:

1 **On the main Digital Lab screen, click the Build a Roller Coaster Right Now button.**

2 **On the Cart Design page, click the design tools to choose a theme, a main color, and a detail color for your coaster.**

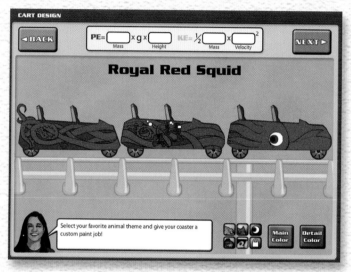

3 **Click the Next button.**

4 **On the Cart Length page, press the − or + button to change the number of cars in the coaster.**

You can have from one to eight cars, each with a mass 100 kg. Each time you change the number of cars, the screen displays your updated coaster and the formula box at the top displays the total mass of the cars.

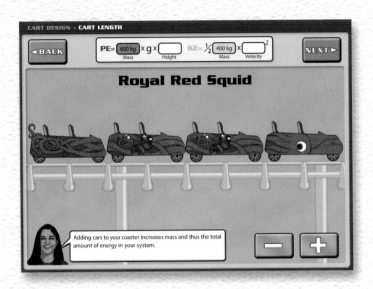

5 Click the Next button.

6 On the Track Design page, build the initial hill.

Click and drag the track node (the black dot); let go when it reaches the height you want. Then click the hill icon next to the track node to select the hill. This first hill should be the highest in your coaster.

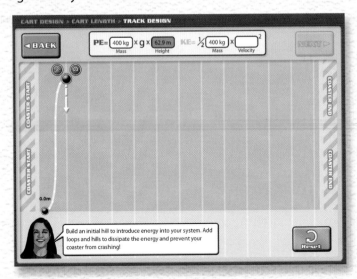

7 Add a new node.

Click the next white line and drag the node to position its height. Then select Hill or Loop. A hill or loop is added according to your selection (you can resize a loop by dragging it). If you want to delete a node, click the red X button.

8 Repeat Step 7 several times to complete the track.

Remember to add both hills and loops in your design. Each hill or loop should be lower than the ones that came before it. The height of each hill or loop is shown in the layout. The last node is the height of the coaster where the ride ends and will roll into the end stop. This is where the riders will get off the coaster.

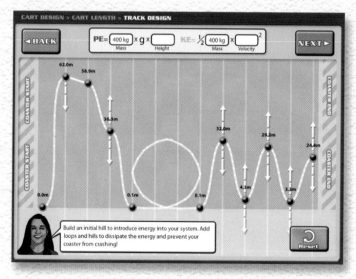

9 Click the Next button.

It's hard to stop the coaster from crashing through the end stop! If you crash, increase the height of the last node to dissipate more energy and decrease kinetic energy at the end of the ride.

10 **On the Coaster Test page, launch your roller coaster to see it in action!**

As your cars move, the indicator at the top of the screen shows the potential energy (PE), kinetic energy (KE), and dissipated energy (DE) at each moment.

If you want to restart the coaster from the start of the track, click the Reset button. You can also click the Pause button to pause the action at any time during the simulation. If your coaster does not work the way you want, click the Back button to return to the Track Design page, where you can change your design.

The formulas for PE and KE are located at the top of the simulation window. Check out an introductory physics book to learn how to compute their values!

11 **When your ride is finished, celebrate the thrill of victory or the agony of defeat.**

A Debrief page appears, where you can review the results of your coaster simulation. The possible outcomes are Crash!, Stuck!, and Success!.

You can move the tracking bar to see the KE, PE, and DE at any point in the ride. The three energies add up to the total energy of the roller coaster system, a number that does not change once the ride is released from its starting point.

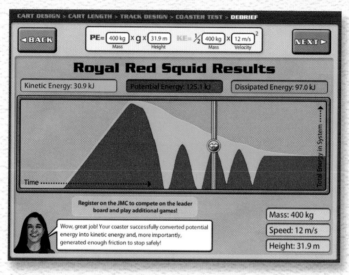

12 **Click the Back button if you want to edit your track or create a different track.**

The Law of Conservation of Energy says that, in a system, energy can't be created or destroyed. But it can change form! Energy is measured in kJ, or kilojoules.

DESIGN YOUR ROLLER COASTER

Once you have created a successful virtual coaster, you'll find that building a real coaster will be easy! Begin by drawing on paper a design for your coaster. This is the design phase of the Engineering Cycle. Think about where you will put hills and loops and what size roller coaster you will build. Decide where you will place your track stop.

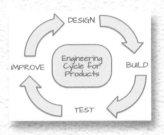

When designing your real coaster, use the same design that you created in your computer simulation.

You will use pipes, flexible tubes, bends, tape, and other materials to build your roller coaster. A marble will act as the cart. While you sketch your design, label the material you plan to use for each section of track. Show the *dimensions* of your track: the *height* of each hill and the *distance* along the ground for each section.

An easy way to plan coaster dimensions is to build your real coaster as a scale model of your computer design. A *scale model* has the same layout as the real object but is larger or smaller in size. Big objects such as roller coasters are scale modeled smaller than their real size. Small objects such as atoms or cells are scale-modeled larger than their real size.

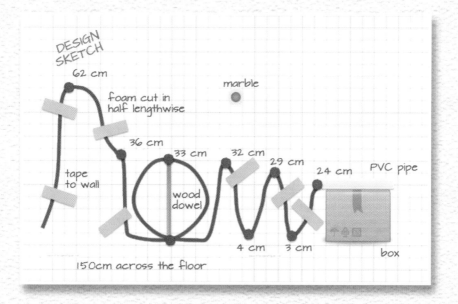

DESIGN SKETCH

62 cm

marble

foam cut in half lengthwise

36 cm

33 cm

32 cm

29 cm

24 cm

PVC pipe

tape to wall

wood dowel

4 cm

3 cm

box

150cm across the floor

On the computer model example, the first hill is 62 meters high, which is about as tall as a 19-story building! Your first hill might be a different height. It will be too hard to build a roller coaster that is many stories high, but it will be easy to build a scale model that is 1/100th as big. This is written as 1:100 scale. Every 1 cm (centimeter) on the coaster will stand for 1 m (meter) on the real coaster (the one created in the computer design). Another way to write this scale is 1 cm = 1 m.

A meter is around the same measurement as a yard. There are 100 centimeters in 1 meter.

BUILD YOUR ROLLER COASTER

Following the design phase of the Engineering Cycle is the build phase. Here, you construct the actual roller coaster.

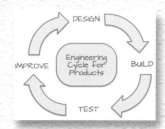

DESIGN

Engineering Cycle for Products

IMPROVE

BUILD

TEST

Begin the build phase by deciding on a *site*, or location, where you will construct your roller coaster:

» An empty wall gives you a blank canvas and a lot of room for taping up coaster parts.

» A staircase or bookcase offers rails or shelves you can attach to, providing support at different heights.

» A coat rack or clothesline provides a place to attach string so that you can make a vertical support for a hill or a loop.

» Plenty of floor space, especially along a hallway, gives you the distance you'll need to build your coaster from start to finish on the ground.

Now you can gather your materials, put on your goggles, and begin the building process. Here are some ways you can work with your materials:

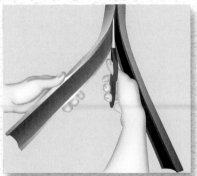

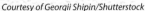

Courtesy of Georgii Shipin/Shutterstock

» Use scissors to cut lengths of foam tubing lengthwise. Each half can be used as a track for the marble coaster. Sections can be made longer by taping cut tubes together, end to end.

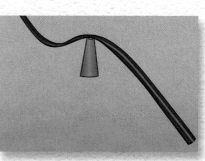

» To create the initial drop, tape the starting coaster section to a wall.

» To elevate a hill, use a box or other support. Place the support under the coaster track. Another option is to bend the foam tubing into a hill and then tape the hill to the wall.

» To make a loop, bend the foam tubing as shown. Tape the ends down for support. You can also add a wooden dowel to support the top of the loop. Another option is to tie a string to the top of the loop and anchor it from above.

» Create additional paths for your marble coaster using PVC tubes. You can use PVC elbows to create a change of direction in your track. PVC tubes can be easily attached to elbow joints. To attach foam tubing to PVC materials, use tape.

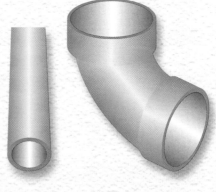

The friction of the foam tubing is greater than the friction of the PVC tubes. This means that the marble coaster slows down more when rolling along the foam.

As you build your coaster, check that each attachment point is secure. The less wobbly the coaster, the better.

TEST YOUR ROLLER COASTER

Now you are in the test phase of the Engineering Cycle for products! Place the marble at the start of your coaster, release it, and observe how it performs. Evaluate how it moves over different sections of the track.

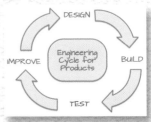

In your design notebook, note any locations where the marble coaster flies off the track, fails to continue moving along the track, or gets stuck. As you observe the performance of your coaster, perform these steps on your design sketch:

1 For a track section where the coaster works well, circle it and put a star next to it.

Note that this is something you should repeat!

2 For a track section that sort of worked, underline it and note how it was partly successful. Also write down how you would try to improve it next time.

3 For a track section that failed, place an X through it and note why you don't recommend repeating it.

The observations you make and write down regarding how well each section works will help you make improvements in the next phase of the Engineering Cycle.

IMPROVE YOUR ROLLER COASTER

Revising, or changing, your design to make it work better is what you do during the improve phase of the Engineering Cycle. The experience you gain from testing your roller coaster gives you the information you need to make improvements.

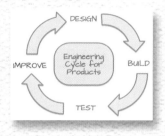

In this phase of the Engineering Cycle, your goal is to learn from what worked and what did not work. Then you can repeat your successes and change the choices that failed.

ENTERTAINMENT ENGINEERING AND THE IRON TRIANGLE

As you complete your work creating a roller coaster, think about the big picture of working on an entertainment engineering project. As in all engineering projects, the Iron Triangle of Engineering tells us that we can do only two of the following three things: a good job, as fast as we can, for cheap.

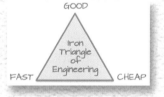

Entertainment engineering projects usually don't have to be completed quickly because they do not meet a critical human need. They also don't necessarily have to be cheap because many of them will end up making money after they are completed. However, the faster they are built, the sooner the owners can begin earning money from them. Entertainment engineering projects, whether they are thrill rides or production shows, must be good or great; otherwise, people will not choose to visit them and spend money on them.

Which two items on the Iron Triangle of Engineering do you believe are most important to an entertainment engineering project, and why?

GOOGLE CARDBOARD: ROLLER COASTER VR

Even if there's not a roller coaster in your town, you can feel as if you're riding one by using Google Cardboard, your mobile phone (iPhone and Android), and a free app!

Courtesy of Andrew Sasaki

Google Cardboard is a cool new virtual reality version of the old-school Mattel View-Master. The software consists of apps that display two images at one time on your mobile phone screen. The images are *stereo,* meaning that they are like the images your eyes see — one image for the left eye and one for the right.

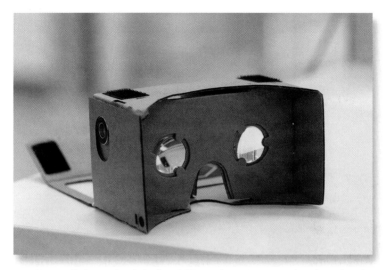

Courtesy of othree — Google Cardboard, CC BY 2.0, https://commons.wikimedia.org/w/index. php?curid=40703922

The hardware puts the images together digitally so that what you see through the viewer feels like the three-dimensional real world. Then it repeats this process thousands of times to create a stereo image for every direction you look. Google Cardboard is better than 3D because when you turn your head, the images change just like you're in the real world. Check out the free apps for Google Cardboard at the App Store and Google Play.

You can purchase a viewer for less than $10, or you can download and build your own viewer using simple, free plans online at www.google.com/get/cardboard/get-cardboard/.

APPENDIX COOL TOOLS (AND MORE!)

LOOKING FOR SOME ADDITIONAL WAYS TO CONTINUE YOUR ENGINEERING EXPLORATIONS? Then check out these cool tools!

Circuit Scribe (www.circuitscribe.com)

Doodle a circuit! Kits contain electrical components, along with a nontoxic silver ink pen for *drawing* wires on paper!

Lego Robotics (www.education.lego.com)

Take kids from Lego architect to Lego mechanical engineers and coders! Use Lego WeDo to build a growling alligator with motorized jaws, or try the new WeDo 2.0 Bluetooth-enabled kits. Experienced junior engineers will want to play with Lego Mindstorms EV3.

Makey Makey (www.makeymakey.com)

Who says user interfaces (UI) have to look like keyboards and touch screens? Re-engineer UI with Makey Makey and turn a banana into a space bar and gobs of Play-Doh into arrow keys!

Ozobot (www.ozobot.com)

Command this tiny robot to follow navigational challenges on your iPad. It's the perfect blend of robotics, coding, and portability.

PBS Kids Engineering Games (www.pbskids.org/games/engineering/)

The website features fun engineering games and puzzles from PBS Kids shows — perfect for the youngest of engineers. Be sure to check out the Design Squad Fidgit Factory and SciGirls AquaBot.

Roominate (www.roominatetoy.com)

This kids' colorful building kit facilitates the construction of everything from dollhouses to elevators, including working lights and motors you can control via iPhone and iPad!

DEDICATION

To Carson and Ian.

ABOUT THE AUTHOR

As a child, Camille McCue, PhD, was fascinated by both her Radio Shack 300-in-1 electronics kit and her weird, applesauce-eating Baby Alive doll. She would have liked to have had an Easy-Bake Oven one Christmas, but forgot all about that upon receiving an Atari 2600. Through endless science fair projects and family crafts, she tinkered, sawed, soldered, photographed, macraméd, and spray-painted in the days before the maker movement was a thing. Camille earned her BA in mathematics at the University of Texas at Austin and her advanced degrees in curriculum and instruction. Her doctoral research at UNLV focused on tween coding.

Camille instructs everything from math enrichment and computer programming to engineering design and physics, both in the classroom and on-air, via television networks, including NASA and PBS. In addition to teaching, Camille has developed and led educational, community outreach programs, including Dawson College Bound and Ready to Learn. She currently directs a Technology Innovation and Integration Initiative, building a giant, school-based fablab — the Startup Incubator at the Adelson Educational Campus in Las Vegas.

Camille and her wonderful husband, Michael, are the proud parents of two remarkable sons, Carson and Ian, and two cuddly beagles, Rocky and Lucy. *Getting Started with Engineering* is Camille's eighth book for Wiley.

AUTHOR'S ACKNOWLEDGMENTS

Thanks to the fabulous team at Wiley for their work in bringing this cool new STEM title to kids everywhere! I'd especially like to thank Steve Hayes, my intrepid executive editor for the past 18 years, as well as extremely talented senior project editor Susan Pink, who has a quick mind for the written word, a kind nudge for a tired author, and a green thumb for the planted flower.

As always, I owe a great deal of thanks to my husband, Michael, and my children, Carson and Ian, for putting up with me during my mad-dash writing sprees. Thanks also to my parents, Beverly and Eric, who cultivated my early interests in STEM. A very special thanks to my son Carson for designing and printing the little green alien ears, and to both my boys for reviewing the Table of Contents to give it an official "thumbs up!" for our readers. Additional appreciation goes to my fabulous students who have tested these projects during school and summer camps.

I am also very grateful to my colleagues Chris Park, Julie Schonfeld, Sylvia Duran, Janelle Boelter, and David James, PhD, who were so kind to serve as technical editors for this book. These practicing engineers reviewed every project before granting their professional stamp of approval! Thank you also to my work teammates Robin Pence, Rachel Ziter, and Yvonne Houy, PhD, for their thoughtful input to Cool Tools. Finally, thank you to Siddique Shaik, production editor, and editorial assistant Kayla Hoffman.

PUBLISHER'S ACKNOWLEDGMENTS

Acquisitions Editor: Steve Hayes

Project Editor: Susan Pink

Production Editor: Siddique Shaik